José Merino
Ex-profesor de Inglés del
Instituto Británico y de la Escuela Oficial
de Idiomas de Madrid

H. Sheerin
Profesor de Inglés de la
Universidad de Valladolid

Phrasal Verbs in Use

Verbos ingleses combinados con partículas

Fourth Edition
(Revised)

ENGLISH LANGUAGE BOOKS
ANGLO DIDACTICA
ANGLO DIDACTICA
PUBLISHING

4ª edición revisada.

Diseño de cubierta: Equipo de diseño de la editorial.
The image used on the cover of this book is from Corel Professional Photos CD-Rom.

Impreso en España.
Printed in Spain.

ISBN: 84-86623-98-7
Depósito legal: M-14.476-2002

Anglo-Didáctica Publishing
C/ Santiago de Compostela, 16 – bajo B
28034 Madrid – Spain.
Tel y fax: (34) 91 378 01 88.
emails: anamerino@worldonline.es
islascies@eresmas.com

Impreso por Fareso, S.A.
Paseo de la Dirección, 5 – 28039 Madrid.

Presentación

Este manual trata de un grupo muy numeroso de verbos ingleses que se caracterizan por ir acompañados de partículas que dan sentidos distintos al verbo. Estos verbos se denominan en inglés *Phrasal Verbs.* Dichas partículas pueden hacer la función de adverbio o de preposición.

El uso correcto de los *Phrasal Verbs* es un aspecto muy importante en la comunicación, pues se emplean constantemente tanto en el lenguaje hablado como escrito, como es el caso, de la prensa.

Aunque este libro es sobre todo una obra de consulta, sugerimos la lectura periódica de las oraciones propuestas, comparando las diferentes partículas de cada verbo y los significados que resultan de su empleo.

Los autores

Contents

Generalidades sobre los *Phrasal Verbs*

Estos verbos, llamados en inglés *Phrasal Verbs,* se emplean profusamente tanto en el lenguaje hablado como en el escrito. Un buen número de los mismos son de uso muy corriente, como por ejemplo:

go off (explotar) **look for** (buscar) **get up** (levantarse)

etc., cuyo uso se prefiere a la versión latina correspondiente. El estudiante debe aprenderlos en una primera etapa y utilizarlos en su vocabulario activo. Otros muchos de estos verbos aparecen con menor frecuencia en el lenguaje coloquial, pero deben conocerse como vocabulario pasivo.

La utilización de gran parte de los verbos acompañados de partículas depende del estilo que desee imprimir el hablante en el discurso. Puede haber hablantes o escritores que prefieran emplear estas formas de origen sajón; otros son partidarios de las formas latinas. En la lista siguiente se comparan ambas:

ORIGEN SAJON	**ORIGEN LATINO**
add in	include
blow up	explode
call on	visit
cut off	disconnect
find out	discover
get away	escape
look on	consider
go for	attack
put back	replace

Las partículas que acompañan a estos verbos cambian, por regla general, el sentido de los mismos.

Pueden distinguirse tres casos:

A) La partícula modifica el sentido del verbo con un matiz adverbial, por ejemplo: **put on** = ponerse (**put** = poner; **on** = encima).

B) La partícula sirve para dar énfasis, por ejemplo: **eat up** = comérselo todo (**up,** en este caso, se emplea con idea de completar la acción).

C) Verbo y partícula unidos adquieren un significado completamente distinto del que tienen por separado, por ejemplo: **bring up** = criar (**bring** = traer; **up** = arriba).

Las partículas más corrientes que sirven para formar estos verbos son las siguientes:

about across after along around at away back by down for forward in into of off on out over round through to under up upon without

Algunas de las ideas básicas que conllevan estas partículas son:

about
a) **De acá para allá:** He went about like a drunken man.
b) **Consigo (con uno mismo):** He always carried a rabbit's foot about with him for luck.

across
Idea de casualidad: Look in that drawer and see if you can come across the document.

after
a) **Tras, en pos de:** The police are after him.
b) **Acerca de:** I met Jones in the street, but I completely forgot to ask after his wife.
c) **Idea de vigilar:** Jane looks after the children in the evening.

along
a) **Idea de desplazarse a corta distancia:** Go along to the shop and buy a packet of salt, please.
b) **Idea de acudir:** You go ahead and find a good table; I`ll be along in a minute.
c) **Idea de congeniar:** He gets along well with his in-laws.

around
a) **De acá para allá:** He gets around a lot on his little motorbike.
b) **Idea de divulgarse:** The news got around that there was going to be a takeover.

at
Idea de atacar: Suddenly the men came at him with knives in their hands.

away
a) **Idea de alejar(se):** The wind blew the mist away from the mountain.
b) **Idea de llevarse:** He carried away our computer and never gave it back.
c) **Idea de desprenderse:** When the wing came away from the toy aeroplane, he fixed it with glue.
d) **Idea de menguar, aminorar:** Attendance at our meetings has dropped away a lot in the past few months.
e) **Idea de marcharse:** She told him to go away and never to come back.

back
a) **Hacia atrás:** Not many men comb their hair back nowadays.
b) **Idea de regresar:** We leave tomorrow and get back on the 30th.

c) **Idea de restituir:** The police gave the bicycle back to my son.
d) **Idea de volver a poner:** Put it back where you found it.
e) **Idea de atrasar:** My watch is fast; I'll put it back an hour.
f) **Idea de aplazar:** He put back his return by one week.

by a) **Idea de transcurrir el tiempo:** The years go by and things don't change.
b) **De acuerdo con:** He always goes by the rules.

down a) **Idea de bajar:** They were having a party in the flat below, so they asked me down.
b) **Idea de cerrar:** The cinema closed down last month.
c) **Hacia abajo:** The tree bent down before the strong wind.
d) **Idea de derribar:** The poplar tree was blown down by the wind in the night.
e) **Idea de bajar algo:** He took a box down from the top shelf.

for a) **Idea de atacar:** The dog came for him with its teeth bared.
b) **Idea de atención:** The dog listened for the sound of his master's car.
c) **Idea de representación:** EU stands for European Union.

in a) **Idea de meter:** My mother brought the geraniums in as the night was cold.
b) **Idea de entrar:** She invited him in to have a cup of coffee.

into **Idea de investigar:** The police are looking into the man's past.

of **Acerca de:** Let's talk of something pleasant.

off a) **Idea de desprenderse:** The catch came off the window when I was opening it.
b) **Idea de desconectar:** They cut off the phone when he didn't pay the bill.
c) **Idea de cortar:** He cut off the end of the banana, which was rotten.
d) **Idea de marcharse, alejarse:** He went off without saying goodbye.
e) **Idea de apagar, cerrar (un interruptor):** Switch off the light, please.

on a) **Idea de continuar:** Go on speaking, please.
b) **Idea de ocurrir:** There is a fight going on down the street.
c) **Idea de encender, abrir (un interruptor):** I switched on the light at five o'clock.
d) **Sobre:** They fell on the enemy and routed them.

out

a) **Idea de sacar:** When he brought out the knife, everybody fell silent.
b) **Idea de salir:** Are you going out tonight or do you prefer to stay at home?
c) **Fuera:** I'm afraid Mr Jones is out today; can I help you?
d) **Idea de apagar o estar apagado:** Is the light out?
e) **Idea de extinguirse:** Many species of wild animals and birds are dying out due to indiscriminate killing.

over

a) **Idea de acabar:** The holidays are over, so it's back to work again now.
b) **Idea de cruzar:** This road goes over the moor.
c) **Idea de rebosar:** The saucepan boiled over and put out the gas.
d) **Por encima de:** The boy jumped over the wall without trouble.

round

a) **Idea de rodear:** The students drew round the teacher attentively while he began the experiment.
b) **Idea de agruparse:** All the people drew round to listen to the speaker.
c) **Idea de pasar algo de una persona a otra:** The letter was sent round the office for all to read.
d) **Idea de acudir desde un lugar cercano:** My neighbour came round for a drink after dinner.

through

A través de: She came through the test very successfully.

to

a) **Idea de resolver un asunto:** I'll see to this matter next week, when I have more time.
b) **Idea de alcanzar:** When they got to the frontier, they were stopped by an armed guard.

under

a) **Abajo:** A torpedo hit the ship and she was sent under.
b) **Debajo:** The animal got under the fence by burrowing.

up

a) **Arriba:** She looked up from her book and smiled.
b) **Idea de terminar completamente:** It's getting late; drink up and let's go.

upon

a) **Contra:** Three ruffians set upon the newcomer and beat him senseless.

b) **Idea de descubrir:** The driver came upon a lad hiding in the lorry.

without

Idea de privación: If there's no wine, we'll just have to do without.

Los *Phrasal Verbs* cuya partícula actúa como adverbio pueden clasificarse en:

a) **Transitivos**; b) **Intransitivos**.

a) **Transitivos** (llevan objeto directo). La partícula puede ir detrás del verbo o detrás del objeto directo. Ejemplos:

I took **down** the notes.
(**down** está detrás del verbo *took*)

I took the notes **down**.
(**down** detrás del objeto directo *the notes*)

He switched **off** the light.
(**off** está detrás del verbo *switched*)

He switched the light **off**.
(**off** está detrás del objeto directo *the light*)

Téngase en cuenta que:

* Si el objeto directo es un pronombre, la partícula se coloca siempre detrás de éste:

I took them **down**.
(**down** va detrás del pronombre *them*)

I switched it **off**.
(**off** va detrás del pronombre *it*)

* Si se desea dar énfasis al objeto directo, o si éste se compone de varias palabras, la partícula va detrás del verbo. Ejemplos:

I took **down** the notes that he dictated.
(**down** está delante del objeto directo *the notes that he dictated)*

He switched **off** the light in the dining-room.
(**off** está delante del objeto directo *the light in the dining-room)*

* Si el verbo está en forma pasiva, la partícula aparece detrás del verbo. Ejemplos:

The notes were taken **down**.
(**down** está detrás de la forma pasiva *were taken*)

The light was switched **off**.
(**off** está detrás de la forma pasiva *was switched*)

b) **Intransitivos** (no llevan objeto directo). La partícula va detrás del verbo. Ejemplos:

He went **off** as soon as he saw me.
(**off** está detrás del verbo *went*)

Come **in** and take a seat, please.
(**in** está detrás del verbo *come*)

Nótese que en exclamaciones, la partícula puede ir delante del sujeto cuando el verbo indica movimiento. Por ejemplo:

Off he went!
In she walked!

Los *Phrasal Verbs* cuya partícula actúa de preposición llevan un sustantivo detrás de la misma. En estos ejemplos, el sustantivo aparece señalado en negrita.

He came down **the street**.
They went into **the problem** very thoroughly.

Como se ha dicho anteriormente, las partículas que acompañan a los verbos pueden ser adverbios o preposiciones. A continuación damos unos ejemplos para ilustrar este punto.

Se nota que la partícula es adverbial porque puede ir delante o detrás de un objeto directo, por ejemplo:

He put **on** his hat o también: He put his hat **on**

lo que no ocurre cuando se trata de una partícula que es preposición, por ejemplo:

He came **down** the street y no: "He came the street **down**."

En los ejemplos siguientes, se pone de manifiesto que una misma partícula puede actuar como adverbio o preposición:

about (adv.): Stop fooling **about** and get on with your work!
(prep.): She asked **about** my daughter's new job.

across (adv.): The street was dangerous, but a young man kindly helped Mr Jones **across**.
(prep.): It is difficult to get **across** this street at this time.

by (adv.): The years go **by** and things don't change.
(prep.): He goes **by** the name of Tubby.

off (adv.): He had taken his coat **off** to work in the garden.
(prep.): Keep **off** the grass.

through (adv.): First you should read the manual **through** carefully.
(prep.): He searched **through** the papers to find the will.

Acentuación de los *Phrasal Verbs*

He aquí las variaciones que se observan con respecto a la acentuación de las partículas tanto adverbiales como prepositivas:

SE ACENTUAN:
a) Cuando acompañan a verbos intransitivos. Por ejemplo:

The 'cars 'drove '**by**.
He 'came '**in** and 'sat '**down**.
His 'eyes 'lit '**up**.

b) Cuando acompañan a verbos transitivos y el objeto directo es un pronombre:

He 'wrote it '**down**.
'Switch it '**off**.
He 'made it '**up**.

c) Cuando el verbo está en forma pasiva, por ejemplo:

The 'notes were 'taken '**down**.
His 'mind was 'made '**up**.
The 'tap was 'turned '**on**.

NO SE ACENTUAN:
a) Cuando acompañan a verbos transitivos y van detrás del objeto directo. Ejemplo:

He 'put his 'hat **on**.
She 'switched the 'light **off**.
'Jane 'made her 'mind **up**.

b) Hay una tendencia a acentuar la partícula adverbial si el objeto directo se compone de varias sílabas y el acento recae en la primera, por ejemplo:

She 'switched the 'television '**off**.

Relación alfabética de los *Phrasal Verbs* en contexto

A

account for **dar cuenta de:** You must account for the money spent.
explicar: Nobody could account for his sudden disappearance.

act for **representar (a alguien):** As the manager is ill today, I'll ask Mr Jones to act for him.

act on **influir sobre:** Do you think this medicine will act on his nerves?
actuar de acuerdo con: I told him to act on my instructions.

act out **representar:** He acted out the comedy of the misunderstood genius to the bitter end.

act up **doler (una parte del cuerpo):** My arm was better after the operation, but it has been acting up again.

act up to **obrar de acuerdo con:** Dolly acted up to her husband's advice.

act upon **influir sobre:** Do you think this medicine will act upon his nerves?
actuar de acuerdo con: I told him to act upon my instructions.

add in **incluir:** Don't forget to add me in for the course.

add up **sumar:** Have you added the bill up yet?

add up to **ascender a (una suma):** The bill added up to 200 euros.
reducirse a: It all adds up to this: the report is false.

answer back **responder (de forma insolente):** Don't answer me back!

answer for **responder de:** You must admit that I can't answer for her actions.

answer up **responder (con claridad):** Answer up; the teacher can't hear you properly.
responder (sin vacilar): You must answer up when the judge asks you a question.

apply for **solicitar, pedir:** Robert Brown is thinking of applying for the directorship.

argue back **llevar la contraria:** Whenever I express an opinion, your sister Betty argues back.

argue out **debatir a fondo (un asunto):** Bill, Jack and Roger argued the matter out and at last they agreed to take immediate action.

argue out of **persuadir (a alguien) para que no haga algo:** Jim's parents had to argue him out of buying a motorbike.

ask about **preguntar por (algo):** She asked about my daughter's new job.
indagar acerca de: The police asked him about his movements on the night of the crime.

ask after **preguntar por (la salud de alguien):** I met Jones in the street, but I completely forgot to ask after his wife.

ask along **invitar (de manera informal):** Ask your cousin along, if you like.

ask away **preguntar (al azar):** There must be lots of things you'd like to know about the job, so ask away!

ask back **volver a invitar:** They were so pleased with the singer's performance that they asked him back for the next concert.

ask down **pedir (a alguien) que baje:** They were having a party in the flat below, so they asked me down.

ask for **preguntar por (alguien):** Has anyone asked for me?
pedir: I'll ask my father for some money.

ask in **invitar (a alguien) a entrar:** Don't keep Johnny standing at the door; ask him in.
pedir (a alguien) que entre: Ask him in; I want to talk to him.

ask on **seguir preguntando:** Ask on; the question and answer session isn't due to end for ten minutes yet.

ask out **invitar (a alguien) a salir:** My parents-in-law asked us out last night and we all went to the new French restaurant.

ask over **invitar (a alguien) a casa:** I would ask you over for coffee but the plumber is coming today.

ask round **invitar (a alguien) a casa :** Betty asked me round for coffee last Saturday.

ask to **invitar (a alguien):** Tom asked Molly to dinner last night.

ask up **pedir (a alguien) que suba:** When he took her home, she asked him up for a coffee.

auction off **subastar:** All her paintings were auctioned off.

B

back away **retroceder:** When the woman attacked him with her umbrella, he backed away and tried to defend himself.

back away from **no estar dispuesto a considerar una idea:** I realized that Mr Brown was backing away from the idea.

back down **volverse atrás:** He was on the point of buying the car, but at the last minute he backed down.
ceder: The manager saw that I stood firm and wouldn't back down.

back onto **lindar con:** Their house is not very comfortable since it backs onto the railway.

back out **volverse atrás:** She backed out of the marriage when she heard he had another girlfriend.
retirarse: They backed out of the fight when they saw the police arriving.
salir reculando: We backed out of the garage.

back up **apoyar:** I shan't be able to do the job unless you back me up.
recular: The car backed up the hill a little and then turned and went away in the opposite direction.

bail out **pagar fianza:** He spent the night in the police station for drunken driving, but he was bailed out the next day by his lawyer.
lanzarse en paracaídas: The pilot had to bail out when the fighter plane was hit by enemy fire.
achicar (el agua): When their boat sprung a leak, they bailed out the water with a can.

bank on **contar con:** You can bank on Jim's coming to the party; he would not miss it for anything.

bargain away **pasar el tiempo discutiendo sobre un precio:** I saw some people spending hours in the market bargaining away over the different products.
sacrificar por poco a cambio: For such a small benefit I will not bargain away my freedom.

bargain for **discutir sobre el precio de algo:** The man bargained for the painting.
contar con: That's more than we bargained for.

bargain on **prever:** I didn't bargain on it raining, so I didn't take my umbrella.

be about **estar a mano:** As there wasn't a scalpel about, the surgeon had to perform the operation with a knife.
ocuparse de: The boss told them to be about their work and stop wasting time.
tratarse de: What's the play about?

be after **ir tras de:** The police are after him.

be along **ir, acudir:** You go ahead and find a table; I'll be along in a minute.

be at **estar haciendo algo:** She is at her knitting again.

be back **estar de vuelta:** I'll be back at seven o'clock.

be behind with **atrasarse con:** Andy can't go to the dance tonight; he is behind with his work.

be down on **tener manía:** The boss is always down on me.

be for **estar a favor de:** Are you for the plan or against it?

be for it **ganársela:** You'll be for it if you contradict the boss.

be in **estar (en casa, en la oficina):** When I answered the phone, a man's voice asked if my father was in.
ser elegido: The new government is in for a five-year term.

be in for **estar expuesto a:** You'll be in for trouble if you don't watch your words.
entrar en (una competición): All those who can are going to be in for the races.
estar amenazado por: We soon realized that we were in for a storm.

be in for it **ganársela:** You'll be in for it if your wife knows you've spent all the money on drink.

be in on **estar en (el secreto):** We were in on the secret but we kept our mouths shut.

be in with **estar a bien con:** You should always be in with the boss.

be off **marcharse:** I must be off now; it's very late.
estar apagado o cerrado: Is the gas off?
quedar aplazado: The meeting is off due to the bad weather.
estropearse (un alimento): The cream was off because of the heat.

estar agotado (en un restaurante): All the items on the menu were off except fish and chips.

be on **estar encendido (o abierto):** Is the light on?

be on at **tenerla tomada con:** The woman next door is always on at her husband. She doesn't give him a moment's peace.

be out **estar fuera (de casa, oficina):** I'm afraid Mr Jones is out today. Can I help you?
estar apagado: Is the light out?

be out for **estar empeñado en conseguir:** She is out for a husband with a lot of money.

be out of **no tener (por haberse agotado):** The shop was out of bread over the weekend.

be over **estar terminado:** The holidays are over, so it's back to work again!

be through **estar enfadado:** Michael and Jane are through; they have broken off their engagement.

be under **estar a las órdenes de:** The soldiers were under Captain Smith.

be up **estar levantado:** The farmer is usually up with the lark.
haber terminado (el tiempo): Time is up! Stop writing and hand in your exams!

be up against it **estar en una situación apurada:** He knew he was up against it when his opponent drew a knife from his pocket.

be up and about **estar recuperado:** He's been down with the "flu" lately, but he's up and about again now.

be up and down **ir tirando (hablando de la salud):** When they asked him how he was feeling, he replied: "Up one day and down the next."

be up in **ser experto en:** Tom's well up in organic chemistry; he's recently published a book.

be up to **estar tramando:** Those two are up to something; they're always whispering.
estar capacitado: It's a difficult deal to pull off, but he's up to it as he has a lot of experience.
ser responsabilidad o decisión (de uno): It's up to you whether you want to come to the party dressed as a Red Indian chief.

bear away **alejarse (un buque):** The warship bore slowly away from the coast.
llevarse (un premio): The Midland pair bore away the top prizes in the dance competition.

bear back **retroceder:** The solitary horseman bore back at full speed when he saw the bandits.

bear down **vencer (una oposición):** They bore down all opposition and eventually got what they wanted.

bear down on **acercarse a:** The column bravely stood its ground as the opposing forces bore down on it.

bear off **alejarse (un buque):** The troopship bore off under full steam.
llevarse (un premio): The clever girl bore off the prize.

bear out **confirmar:** The detective's suspicions were borne out when he saw a blood stain on the suspect's coat.

bear up **mantenerse firme:** He bore up well under questioning and didn't tell them anything.

beat about for **buscar apuradamente:** The landlord was beating about for an excuse to evict the tenant.

beat away **ahuyentar (a golpes):** The old man beat the savage dog away with his cane.

beat back **rechazar (a golpes):** The defenders beat the attackers back three times before help came.

beat down **regatear (el precio):** The gypsy asked seventy pounds for the horse, but the farmer beat him down to fifty.
derribar (a golpes): The boxer beat his opponent down to his knees with hard blows.

beat off **rechazar (a golpes):** The small group of soldiers couldn't beat off the attack of the well-organized enemy.

beat up **batir (huevos):** Mary is in the kitchen beating eggs up for an omelette.
dar una paliza: The cowardly youths beat the old man up when they found he had no money.
navegar (contra el viento): The steamer had to beat up The Channel against a fierce gale.

beg off **excusar (de un castigo):** Mr Wilson means to punish Jim, but Mr Toon, his teacher, is going to try to beg him off.
pedir permiso (para salir del trabajo): I begged the day off from work as I wanted to see the match.

bend down **inclinarse:** The tree bent down before the strong wind.

bend over **inclinarse sobre:** He bent over the engine of the car to see why it would not work.

bent on **resuelto a:** They are bent on sending their son to a public school.

bid up **pujar (en una subasta):** Everybody bid up and the picture sold for a high price.

bind down **sujetar:** The farmer bound the hay ricks down with ropes when the storm came.
limitar: He was bound down by a lot of rules and regulations.

bind up **vendar:** The nurse bound up the man's injured arm.
atar: The intruders bound the watchman up before robbing the factory.

bite into **corroer:** In a short time the acid bit into the iron.

bite off **abarcar más de lo que se puede:** He bit off too much when he took on the extra work.

bite on **empezar a morder:** He bit on the apple, forgetting for a moment his bad tooth.

block up **obstruir:** The tea leaves blocked up the drain pipe and he had to call the plumber.

blot out **oscurecer:** The sun was blotted out by the windstorm.
borrar: He tried to blot out her image by thinking of someone else.

blow away **llevarse (el viento):** The wind blew the mist away from the mountain top.
disiparse: The cloud of dust blew away as quickly as it had formed.

blow down **derribar (el viento):** The poplar tree was blown down by the wind in the night.

blow in **caer hacia adentro (por una explosión):** The great door was blown in by the terrible explosion.
aparecer inesperadamente: Harvey blew in when we were least expecting him.
entrar (por la acción del viento): When she opened the door a swirl of snowflakes blew in.

blow into **soplar dentro de (algo):** The boy blew into the balloon to inflate it.
aparecer inesperadamente (en un lugar): Harvey blew into town when we were least expecting him.

blow off **volarse:** The wind blew the papers off his desk and they were never seen again.
quitar soplando: He blew the dust off the old book before opening it.

blow out **apagar soplando:** He blew out the candle and settled down to sleep.
inflar: The wind blew the sails out and the boat went faster.
fundirse (un fusible): When all the fuses blew out, the building was left in darkness.
reventar: The tyre blew out as we were driving to the cinema.

blow over **disiparse:** The thunderstorm blew over pretty soon.
olvidarse: When the cause of the dispute had blown over, they shook hands.

blow up **hacer volar:** The commando group blew the bridge up with dynamite.
inflar: The team blew the football up before the match.
explotar: The boiler blew up and several people were injured.
regañar: When I arrived home late, my father blew me up.
desatarse (una tormenta): A severe storm blew up and lasted for two days.
perder los estribos: This bad news was the last straw for George: he blew up with curses right and left.
arreciar (el viento): The wind freshened and blew up into a steady gale.

boil away **evaporarse:** When the water boiled away, there were grains of salt left at the bottom of the test tube.

boil down **consumirse:** They boiled the liquid down until it formed a thick soggy mass.

boil down to **reducirse a:** It all boils down to this: we need more money for the job.

boil over **enfadarse:** The boss boiled over when the men spoke badly of him.
rebosar (por ebullición): The saucepan boiled over and put the gas out.

bolt in **encerrar (con cerrojo):** They closed the stable door and bolted the horse in.

bolt out **no dejar entrar:** He returned home late and found he was bolted out for the night.

book in **hacer una reserva (en un lugar):** It's a popular hotel: you ought to book in soon to be sure of a room.

book out **pagar y marcharse (de un hotel):** We'd like to book out before eight o'clock in the morning.

book down **apuntar:** He was booked down for several events he didn't take part in.

book up **comprometerse:** Sorry, but I can't come because I'm already booked up for that day.

boss about **mangonear:** Don't boss me about; I don't work for you.

bound off **alejarse saltando:** The rabbit bounded off when it saw the dog.

bound up in **absorto en:** He's very bound up in his studies and has no time for anything.

bow down to **doblegarse a:** All the people in that country bowed down to the tyrant.

bow out **despedir (con una reverencia):** The Japanese delegation bowed ceremoniously out of the conference room.

break away **soltarse:** The prisoner broke away and escaped when he was being taken to the police station.

break down **derribar:** The firemen broke the door down with sledge-hammers.
averiarse: Our car broke down when we were coming back from holiday.
romperse (negociaciones): Negotiations have broken down without any hope of an agreement.
romper a llorar: The prisoner broke down and confessed when he was confronted with the evidence.
vencer (una oposición): Mr Toon broke down all opposition.

break in **forzar la entrada:** The man waited until it was dark before breaking in.
irrumpir: When the bank doors were opened an impatient crowd broke in demanding their money.
interrumpir: It is discourteous to break in when someone is speaking.
domar: The farmer spent a long time trying to break the horse in.
forzar: As he had lost his key he broke the door in with his shoulder.

break into **prorrumpir en:** The crowd broke into excited cheering when they heard the news.
entrar (por la fuerza) en: The thief broke into the bank and stole 20,000 pounds.
partir (en trozos): She broke the loaf of bread into pieces, one for each child.

break off **dejar de trabajar por un momento:** Let's break off and have a glass of beer.
partir (romper): He broke off a bit of chocolate and gave it to her.
romper (relaciones): The two countries have broken off diplomatic relations and recalled their ambassadors.
dejar de hablar de repente: He was telling me a joke but he broke off when he saw the boss coming.

break out **estallar (una guerra):** War broke out between the two countries.
declararse (una epidemia): A typhoid epidemic broke out without warning.
fugarse: A group of prisoners broke out last night.
brotar: Curious red spots broke out all over his skin.
exclamar: "My God", he broke out, "the nerve of some people!"

break out into **proferir:** He broke out into abuse when they didn't give him the money.
echarse a llorar: She broke out into loud wails of grief.

break through **abrirse paso por:** He broke through the crowd gathered at the scene of the accident.
aparecer (el sol, la luna): At last the sun broke through after a month of heavy rain.

break up **desguazar:** All these old cars will be broken up for their parts.
desmenuzar: She broke the bread up into crumbs to throw to the birds.
terminar el curso escolar: School breaks up at the end of next week.
disgregarse: The ice sheet broke up into little particles.
hacer añicos: He broke up the giant toadstool with blows of his stick.
hacerse pedazos: The ship broke up against the rocks.
levantarse (una reunión): The meeting broke up at about one.
dispersar: The police broke the demonstration up.
separarse (un matrimonio): People say that Tom and Molly are breaking up.

breathe in **aspirar:** I like to breathe in the fresh air of the countryside.

breathe out **espirar:** Your chest sinks in when you breathe out.

bring about **ocasionar:** A great change in thinking was brought about because of this book.
virar: The captain ordered the ship brought about and headed for the port.
llevar a cabo: The new director brought about a complete revival of the company.

bring along **educar:** They are bringing my son along very well in that school.
traer consigo: Bring your daughter along the next time you come.

bring away **llevarse:** He brought away a beautiful bride and the envy of the township.

bring back **devolver:** The money was brought back last week.
traer a la memoria: That song brings back some happy memories.
traer de regreso: The astronauts brought back a piece of moon rock.

bring down **abatir (de un disparo):** The hunter brought the animal down with one shot.
hacer descender: That scandal will soon bring him down from his pedestal.
rebajar (el precio): They brought the price down by more than half.

bring forward **proponer:** Then the chairman brought forward a motion that caused some surprise.
pasar el total de una página a otra: The book-keeper added up the sum and brought the total forward.

bring in **meter:** She brought the geraniums in as the night was cold.
producir (de beneficio): His investments bring him in a pretty penny each month.
servir (a la mesa): When the waiter brought in the dessert, everyone applauded.
ganar (dinero): There are three of them working and bringing in money.
pronunciar (un veredicto): The jury brought in a verdict of "guilty."

bring into **traer (algo) dentro (mencionando el lugar):** Will you bring the tea things into the sitting-room?

bring off **conseguir un éxito:** The new minister brought off a complete reform of the divorce laws.
llevarse: The helicopter brought the men off the sinking ship.

bring on **ocasionar:** His blindness was brought on by too much study.

bring out **publicar:** I hear Faber are bringing out a book of his soon.
sacar: When he brought out the knife everyone fell silent.

hacer salir: He brought the dog out with a sharp whistle.
introducir (en sociedad): Are heiresses brought out in society nowadays?
demostrar: It was brought out in the trial that not all the guilty were in court.
revelar: I think this will be brought out in the near future.

bring over **persuadir:** He didn't like the idea at first but we brought him over.
convertir (a una religión): They brought him over to their persuasion and now he is as zealous as any of them.
traer a casa: Bring your friends over, too; we're having a party!

bring round **traer (desde una corta distancia):** He brought it round when he came.
hacer volver en sí: A whiff of the smelling salts brought her round.
persuadir: With some effort we brought him round to our way of thinking.

bring to **parar (un barco):** The captain brought the boat to and ordered, "Fire!"
hacer volver en sí: A glass of brandy will soon bring him to.

bring under **someter:** In spite of their resistance they were soon brought under.
controlar: The new teacher finds very difficult to bring the children under control.

bring up **educar (criar):** The boy was brought up in France.
parar: He was brought up short when the chairman told him he was speaking out of order.
vomitar: The boy was sick and brought up everything he had eaten.
sacar (un tema): When he brought up the subject of his holidays everybody groaned.
arrimar: Bring your chair up to the fire and sit down.
subir (transitivo): Bring me up a book to read; I can't sleep!
servir (alimentos): They took so long in bringing up the last course that we had begun smoking.

brush aside **rechazar (con desdén):** They brushed all my objections aside and went ahead with the project.

brush off **quitar cepillando:** She brushed the dust off the table with a specially impregnated cloth.

brush over **pintar ligeramente:** He brushed the wall over, since that was all it needed.

brush up **repasar:** You'll have to brush up your French before the exam.
lustrar: She ordered the servants to brush up the brasswork.

build up **acumularse:** At this time of the day problems just build up.
aumentar (los ahorros): Their savings built up over the years and they now have a lot put by.
llenar (de edificaciones): There used to be a park here, but now it's all built up.
vigorizar: The doctor gave him a tonic to build up his strength.

build in **empotrar:** All the wardrobes in the bedrooms are built in.

burn away **continuar ardiendo:** The fire is still burning away despite the efforts of the firemen.
consumirse: A part of the document was burned away when he snatched it from the fire.

burn down **arder totalmente (una edificación):** The school burned down two years ago.

burn out **consumirse (el fuego):** The forest fire soon burned itself out.

burn up **quemar (en un montón):** He burnt up all the old letters before he left.
avivarse (el fuego): The fire burned up and cast shadows on the wall.

burst in **entrar apresuradamente:** The door opened and the students burst in.
interrumpir impulsivamente: Then he burst in with another nonsensical remark.

burst into **entrar apresuradamente en:** Suddenly several policemen burst into the room and arrested the poker players.
empezar espontáneamente: My sister Jane burst into song.

burst out **reventar:** The door was burst out by the explosion.
exclamar: "What's the meaning of this?" he burst out.
romper a (reír, llorar): I burst out laughing when I saw her face.
prorrumpir: He burst out into insults when she turned him down.

butter up **adular:** That fellow is always trying to butter the boss up.

button up **abotonar:** Button up your coat; the evening is cool.

buy back **recobrar (por compra):** My father bought this house back from the person he sold it to.

buy off **sobornar:** The Byzantine emperors bought their enemies off rather than have to fight them.

buy out **comprar (un negocio):** The firm was bought out by a multinational.

buy over **sobornar:** The case fell through because some of the witnesses were bought over.

buy up **acaparar:** During the fuel crisis, the public bought up all the bottles of gas we had in the store.

C

call at **hacer una visita corta (a una casa, a una tienda, a correos):** I called at John's but he wasn't in.
hacer escala: The ship calls at Rio on its way to Buenos Aires.

call away **llamar en vano:** Call away! There's no-one to hear you!
mandar (a alguien) que se aleje: The mother called the boy away when she saw him talking to the tramp.
distraer (la atención): He stopped listening as his attention was called away by a familiar sound.

call back **mandar regresar:** She called the boy back as he had forgotten his sandwiches.
volver para hacer una segunda visita: The milkman will call back at any house he missed.
volver a llamar por teléfono: I'll call you back in an hour.

call by **visitar (a alguien al pasar por un lugar):** When you're next in Madrid, please call by.

call down **mandar bajar:** The landlady called the lodger down as his breakfast was ready.
invocar: He called down the heavenly powers to witness he was telling the truth.
llamar (dirigiendo la voz hacia abajo): The woman called down to her husband in the street.

call for **requerir:** The old man called for his hat and cane.
pedir (a gritos): He called for help but no one heard him.
ir o venir a buscar: I'll call for you on my way to the cinema.
exigir: That remark of yours calls for an explanation.

call in **mandar pasar:** The boss told the secretary to call in the next applicant.

invitar a entrar: I was going by the house when they called me in.
hacer una corta visita: I've just called in to see if you want anything.

call off **llamar (para distraer la atención):** The dog was about to attack the man but I called it off.
desistir: They were planning to buy a new house but called it off.
suspender: The open-air concert was called off due to the bad weather.

call on **visitar (a alguien):** Don't forget to call on Tom when you're there.
invitar (a hablar): Everybody called on Mr Jones to make a speech.
exhortar: The politician called on the people of the country to support the government.
llamar (a alguien para que preste un servicio): We'll have to call on him to help us.

call out **gritar:** He called out with pain when the dog bit him.
movilizar: The troops were called out to quell the uprising.
llamar (a alguien para que salga): My son's friend called him out of the house to see his new bicycle.
llamar a voces: He called out the boy's name but there was no answer.

call over **pasar lista:** He called over the names without stopping until he came to Smith.

call up **llamar a filas:** He was called up to do his National Service.
llamar por teléfono: Mildred called me up last night.
mandar subir: They called him up to the third floor to ask him a few questions.
evocar: This song calls up memories of other days.
despertar: The lodger was called up by the landlady at seven o'clock.
invocar (espíritus): Do spiritualists really call up the spirits of the departed?

calm down **calmarse:** She calmed down when I assured her that there was nothing to worry about.

care about **importarle a alguien algo:** I don't care about what the boss thinks.

care for **apetecer:** Would you care for some brandy with your coffee?
cuidar de: She cared for the children while her sister was working.
importarle (a uno): I don't care a straw for your opinion.

carry about **llevar consigo:** He always carried a rabbit's foot about with him for luck.

carry along **persuadir:** She refused to let herself be carried along by his argument.

carry away **llevarse:** He carried away our television set and never gave it back.
llevarse (un premio): Jim and Jean carried away the top prizes for dancing.
entusiasmar: The teacher got so carried away with the subject that he didn't hear the bell.
transportar lejos: The ship carried the emigrants away, and we thought the crisis had passed.

carry back **traer de vuelta:** The slain warriors were carried back to the village for burial.

carry down **bajar (transitivo):** The old woman could not walk and had to be carried down the stairs.

carry forward **arrastrar (una suma):** After adding up the list, he carried the total forward.

carry off **ganar (un premio):** Jean carried off the first prize for the school essay.
morir: He was carried off by an untimely pneumonia.

llevar a cabo: What he had to do was difficult, but he carried it off to perfection.
llevarse (a la fuerza): The pirates invaded the island and carried off hostages.

carry on **continuar (no dejar de):** The foreman told the men to carry on working.
avanzar: It was an exhausting climb but they carried on until they reached the top of the hill.
llevar (una conversación): Can he carry on a conversation in English?
comportarse (de forma rara): Did you notice how the students were carrying on?
perseverar: He is still carrying on with the idea of marrying the girl.

carry out **llevar a cabo (instrucciones):** I want you to carry out my instructions to the letter.
poner en práctica: They carried the plan out successfully.

carry over **arrastrar (una suma):** He added up the figures and carried the total over.
llevarse (a otro lugar): The blacksmith lifted the anvil and carried it over to the other end of the forge.
aplazar: First, they discussed the points carried over from the previous meeting.

carry through **llevar a cabo (a pesar de dificultades):** He managed to carry his plan through despite great difficulties.
sostener: His belief in his own abilities carried him through.
ayudar a alguien en momentos difíciles: His example carried his fellow countrymen through the war.

carry up **subir (transitivo):** He carried the heavy suitcases up the stairs.

cash in **cambiar por dinero:** I intend to cash my shares in at the end of two years.

cast about **buscar con afán:** He was always casting about for a way to get invited to parties.

cast away **arrojar (algo a la costa el mar):** Robinson Crusoe was cast away on a desert island.

cast back **tratar de recordar:** He cast back but he couldn't remember the details.

cast down **deprimido:** Albert was very cast down when he heard the bad news.
bajar (los ojos): When Jane heard Tim's words, she cast her eyes down modestly.

cast off **zarpar:** The ferry cast off and began the crossing half an hour late.
desechar: He is very lucky in the way he can cast off all his worries.
terminar una labor de punto: When she finished knitting she cast off and put the needles away.
dejar (malas compañías): The magistrate advised him to cast off all his former associates if he really wanted to reform.

cast on **empezar una labor de punto:** When you begin knitting you cast on by putting the first stitches on to the needle.

cast out **tirar:** My husband says that we really must cast out all these old newspapers.
desterrar: He was cast out and ordered never to return to the tribe.

cast up **calcular:** The accountant had to cast up the accounts.
vomitar: He cast up all he had eaten.
arrojar (algo a la costa el mar): The man's body was cast up onto the shore.

catch on **hacerse popular:** The new fashion is beginning to catch on.
entender: I tried to show him discreetly what he had done wrong, but he didn't catch on.

catch up **alcanzar:** They caught us up before we reached the town.

catch up on **ponerse al día:** I've got a lot of reading to catch up on in the holidays.

catch up with **alcanzar:** As we drove faster, we caught up with them before long.
ponerse a nivel de: The teacher told him to work harder if he wanted to catch up with the rest of the class.

chance on **encontrar por casualidad:** I chanced on a pharmacy on my way back to the hotel and at once bought the tablets I needed.

check in **registrar la entrada:** Passengers must check their luggage in before boarding the plane.

check out **registrar la salida:** He checked out of the hotel at ten in the morning.
hacer una comprobación: The bank checked me out before allowing me a mortgage.

check up on **comprobar (a conciencia):** The police are checking up on his movements.

cheer on **animar (con vítores):** The crowd cheered on their favourite team.

cheer up **animarse:** He cheered up considerably when he heard the good news.

chime in with **estar de acuerdo con:** Luckily, his ideas chimed in perfectly with ours.
entrar en la conversación: Suddenly Joyce chimed in with "I've been there, too!"

choke down **refrenar:** He choked down his anger and didn't say a word.

choke up **atascarse:** The pipe was choked up with sand.

chop off **cortar (con hacha):** The woodman chopped off all the branches of the tree.

chop up **cortar (en trocitos):** She chopped the onion up into small pieces.

clean down **lavar (un coche):** The man cleaned the car down with a sponge and a bucket of water.

clean out **vaciar (algo para limpiarlo):** She cleaned the cupboard out and then put everything back in its place.
limpiar (una habitación): We spent the whole day cleaning out the room that the squatters had used as a kitchen.

clean up **asear (un lugar):** The maid cleaned up after the guests had left.
terminar con: The new mayor cleaned up the gangster element.
ganar: He cleaned up a tidy sum of money in the card game.

clear away **disiparse:** When the smoke had cleared away they contemplated the massacre.
quitar (cosas que estorban): She cleared away the dishes before serving dessert.

clear off **marcharse (largarse):** The barman told the drunkard to clear off.
echar (a alguien): The farmer cleared the boys off his premises.
quitar (lo que estorba): Clear the table off, we're going to play cards.

clear out **vaciar:** The secretary cleared out the drawer as she needed somewhere to put her belongings.
marcharse: They cleared out when they saw that trouble was coming.
desalojar: The unruly elements among the audience had to be cleared out before the meeting could continue.

clear over **pasarse (un suceso):** We had a small problem with our neighbours but it has cleared over.

clear up **despejarse (el tiempo):** When the bad weather cleared up, they went to the seaside.
aclararse (un misterio): The mystery was cleared up when the weapon was found.

arreglar (asear): The housewife cleared up and washed her hands.
limpiar (un lugar): The workmen forgot to clear up the yard after they had finished.

climb down **descender:** When the fire started, he climbed down the wall by the drain-pipe.

climb up **trepar:** The burglars climbed up by pulling themselves onto the balcony.

clock in **fichar la entrada:** The factory workers clock in at eight o'clock.

clock off **fichar la salida:** There was a line of men waiting to clock off.

clock on **fichar la entrada:** After the office girl clocked on, she hung up her coat.

clock out **fichar la salida:** The men clocked out and filed through the gate.

close down **cerrar (una emisión):** The radio station closes down at midnight.
cerrar (un negocio): The new owner closed the old branch of the business down.

close in **acortarse (los días):** In autumn the days begin to close in.
rodear: The hungry wolves closed in on the man.
encerrar: They closed the calf in the shed.

close up **acercarse:** The ranks of soldiers closed up at the officer's command.
tapar: The mason closed the small window up with cement.
bloquear: The fallen leaves closed the drain up.
cerrar (por una temporada): These beach restaurants close up for the winter season.

cloud over **nublarse:** The day is clouding over; it looks as if we are going to have rain.

cloud up **nublarse:** It suddenly clouded up and blew a storm from the west.

comb back **peinarse hacia atrás:** Not many men comb their hair back nowadays.

comb out **registrar (un lugar):** The police combed out the neighbourhood looking for the thief.

come about **ocurrir:** It came about that the entire country was hit by a plague.
rodear: The hungry people came about him begging for bread.

come across **encontrar (por casualidad):** Look in that drawer and see if you can come across the document.
encontrarse con (por casualidad): I was going along the street when I came across John playing a guitar for money.
cruzar: He came across the lake in a little boat.
salir bien: The sketch by the comedy group came across very well.

come after **venir detrás de:** The bull came after the man bellowing and snorting.
venir después de: August comes after July.

come along **acompañar:** If you like I'll come along with you as far as the corner.
ir bien (progresar): The author claims his new book is coming along very well.
venir por: Did you come along by the river on your way here?
darse prisa: Come along, we haven't got all day!
presentarse: You should take every chance that comes along.

come at **abalanzarse sobre:** Suddenly the men came at him with knives in their hands.

come away **desprenderse:** When the wing came away from the toy aeroplane, he fixed it with glue.

venir (con el que habla): "Come away," he said, "there's nothing to keep you here."
marcharse (alejarse): We came away from the meeting feeling that we had learned a lot.

come back **regresar:** My father's away in the town; he's coming back this evening.
venir (a la memoria): The memory of all their happy days together came back to him.

come by **adquirir:** The police wanted to know how he had come by the radio he had in his hand.
pasar por: Come by the house on your way home from work and we can have a drink!

come down **bajar (intransitivo):** This is my son coming down the stairs now.
venir a menos: That once-rich family has come down a lot in the world.
venir de tradición: The peculiar traits of his come down from his grandfather.
caerse: He came down from the top of the tree like a bag of cement.
venir (de la capital): Our friends are coming down from London to visit us.
bajar (los precios): Food prices are rumored to be coming down shortly.

come down on **regañar:** The teacher came down on the boys for laughing in class.
exigir: The debt collector came down on them for payment.
censurar: They came down heavily on him for what he did.

come for **venir por:** I've come for the book you promised to lend me.
atacar: The dog came for him with its teeth bared.

come in **entrar:** She invited him to come in and have a cup of coffee.
ponerse de moda: Long skirts seem to be coming in this winter.
tener cabida: Where does he come in in all this business?

come in for **ser objeto de:** His plan came in for a lot of criticism.
heredar: How much money will he come in for when his aunt dies?
ganarse una bronca: He came in for it when they found out the truth.

come off **resultar:** If everything comes off as expected, he will be happy.
desprenderse (de): The catch came off the window when I was opening it.
caerse (de): He came off the bicycle when he hit the wall.
tener éxito: His attempt to swim the Channel both ways didn't come off.
tener lugar: I believe their wedding is not coming off.
retirar (del cartel): The play, which has been running for six years, is coming off soon.

come on **seguir:** Come on, children: you're getting behind!
progresar: His new book is coming on very well, he says.
sobrevenir: The rain came on when the players were already out on the field.
avanzar: Despite a hail of bullets, the attacking army came on steadily.
aparecer (en el escenario): The audience laughed when the actor came on carrying an umbrella.
empezar: Look, there are flowers all around! Spring is coming on now!

come on to **pasar a (un asunto):** "I'm coming on to that point next," said the president at the meeting.

come out **salir:** Who's that coming out of the house now?
publicarse: When is your next book coming out?
declararse (en huelga): The rail workers are coming out on strike next week.
resultar: It came out more or less as he expected.
presentarse (en sociedad): Lord Robert's daughter is coming out next spring.
quitarse (una mancha): That stain will come out with alcohol.

come over **venir (recorriendo una distancia):** They asked her when she had come over from the States.
cruzar: Did you come over the park on your way here?
cambiar (el tiempo): It suddenly came over stormy.
cambiar (de lugar): Come over to this side of the room; you'll see better.
dejarse persuadir: He came over to our way of thinking.

come round **recobrar el sentido:** When she came round after the operation, she asked for a drink.
venir (de visita): Come round to visit us any evening!
engañar: She came round him in the subtlest way and persuaded him.
cambiar (de parecer): You'll come round to our way of thinking.

come through **venir a través de:** As I was coming through the wood, I saw an old woman picking mushrooms.
autorizar: Permission has finally come through to proceed with the sale.

come to **recobrar el sentido:** After he was knocked out, it was an hour before he came to.
ascender a (una suma): What he spent last month came to twice what he earned.
significar: What you've said comes to this: it's all a pack of lies!

come up **subir (intransitivo):** Come up to bed, children. It's nine o'clock!
brotar: The crocus is one of the first flowers to come up in spring.
ingresar (en la universidad): When Jones came up to university, he was a hard-working chap.
surgir: Something unexpected has come up, so I'm afraid I can't go.
venir (a la ciudad): When are you coming up to London next?
emerger: The moon came up over the horizon and was reflected in the water.

hacer una visita: Please come up and see us some time.

come up against **encontrarse con:** I came up against a difficult problem I couldn't solve.
enemistarse con: Old Grimes is not the sort of person I'd like to come up against.

come up to **acercarse:** A man came up to me in the street and asked me for money.
estar a la altura de: His latest book doesn't come up to his earlier ones.
subir a : Will you come up to the top of the tower with me?

come up with **sugerir, proponer (de forma inesperada):** Brian came up with the perfect solution to the problem.

come upon **encontrar (por casualidad):** Who do you think I should come upon there but our friend Macey!
atacar: The bandits came upon Mr Brown with clubs and knives.
encontrar (de repente): I suddenly came upon the answer when I least expected it.

conjure away **hacer desaparecer:** She managed to conjure away all his ample fortune in one year.

conjure up **evocar:** This conjures up visions of palm trees and sandy beaches.
invocar: The medium conjured up the spirit of the dead man.

cook up **maquinar:** Those two must be cooking something up; they are always whispering together.
cocinar algo deprisa: Can you cook up a simple egg dish for me tonight?

cool down **calmarse:** Cool down; you shouldn't get excited so quickly!
enfriarse: The dish is still too hot to touch; leave it for several minutes to cool down.

cool off **enfriarse:** Let's wait for the engine to cool off.

cork down **tapar (con un corcho):** He corked the liquid down and left it for a week.

cork up **tapar (con un corcho):** You've got to cork up all those bottles before you finish.

count back **contar al revés:** We are in December now; I want you to count back to the tenth of October.

count down **contar hacia atrás:** The scientists counted down from ten to zero and the rocket's engines burst into flame.

count for **contar (ser necesario, importante):** His opinion counts for something; we should listen to it.

count in **incluir:** Count me in for the football match; I'd love to play.

count on **contar con:** We can count on him to help us when we are in need.

count out **contar hasta diez (en boxeo):** The boxer was counted out when he did not get up.
excluir: You can count Peter out; he doesn't like parties.

count over **comprobar un total:** The wardens counted the prisoners over after the escape attempt.

count up **contar:** He was counting up the days until it was holiday time.
sumar: Count up the two lists and add them together.

count up to **contar hasta:** That child is very slow; she can't count up to twenty.

cover over **tapar (cubriendo):** They covered the coffin over and nailed down the lid.

cover up **tapar (para ocultar):** Cover up that hole in the wall; it looks unsightly!

tapar (un asunto para proteger a alguien): Her employers never discovered her thefts because her colleagues covered up for her.

crash into **chocar con:** The car crashed into a lamppost.

cross off **tachar (de una lista):** They crossed off his name when he didn't turn up at the meeting.

cross out **tachar:** He crossed out what he had written and began a new line.

cross over **cruzar:** He crossed over to the other side of the river and began fishing.

crowd in **entrar en tropel (con impaciencia):** The courtroom doors opened punctually and the waiting public crowded in to get good seats.

crowd out **salir en tropel:** When the examination was over, all the students crowded out.

crush up **triturar:** This is a machine for crushing the rock up.

cry back **responder a gritos:** He put his hand to his mouth and cried back across the valley.

cry down **acallar a gritos:** When the politician tried to speak, he was cried down by the crowd.
despreciar: They cried down his efforts as useless.

cry for **pedir a gritos:** He shouted and cried for help but nobody heard him.
llorar por: The child cried for his lost toy.
clamar por: The bloodthirsty crowd cried for vengeance.

cry off **echarse atrás (en un compromiso):** He had agreed to lead the expedition but he cried off at the last moment.

cry on **azuzar:** The group in the street cried the two boxers on.

seguir llorando: The child cried on until someone gave it a sweet.

cry out **gritar (de dolor):** The man cried out with pain when the anvil fell on his foot.
gritar (de emoción): On seeing me safe and well, she cried out with joy.
exclamar: He cried out in amazement when he saw the sight.
pregonar: The street vendor was crying out his wares.

cry out to **clamar:** This crime cries out to heaven for vengeance.

cry over **lamentar:** It's no good crying over something you can't remedy.

cut across **atajar:** He cut across the fields to avoid going round by the road.
cerrar el paso (un coche a otro): I nearly had an accident when a car cut across in front of me.

cut away **marcharse rápidamente:** He cut away without a word when he saw his wife coming.
partir: He cut the hard crust away and ate the bread greedily.

cut back **acortar (gastos):** The chairman said the firm would have to cut back expenses.

cut down **talar:** The early settlers cut down all the virgin forest.
reducir (gastos): The factory will have to cut down on spending and overheads.
morir: He was cut down in the full bloom of his youth.
matar: The invaders cut down their poorly armed opponents.

cut in **interrumpir:** His wife always cuts in when he begins talking about their courtship.
cerrar el paso: You should never cut in after overtaking another vehicle.

cut into **interrumpir (una conversación):** She cut into our conversation without the least apology.

cortar en: Mrs Wilson cut the cake into quarters and shared it equally among the children.

cut off **cortar (el teléfono, el gas):** They cut the phone off when he didn't pay the bill.
cortar: He cut off the end of the banana which was rotten.
aislar: The village was cut off due to the heavy snowstorm.
desheredar: Her family cut her off without a penny when she married the bricklayer.
romper (las relaciones): Why did you cut off all relations like that?
morir: He was cut off in his prime due to a sudden illness.
amputar: The doctor had to cut off the injured miner's leg.
interceptar: One of the wolves cut off the goat's escape while the rest closed in.
hacer callar: Mary Brown, the secretary, always cuts me off when I'm speaking.

cut out **recortar:** Children like cutting out pictures of their favourite footballers.
omitir: I think we should cut out all references to the government in the speech.
cortar (una prenda): The dressmaker cut the dress out before beginning to sew it.
dar forma: I'm going to cut out a ship from this piece of wood.
suprimir: The doctor advised him to cut out smoking and drinking.
abrir (un camino): They cut a path out through the forest.
pararse (de repente): The engine cut out and the car refused to move another inch.

cut out for **nacido para:** It is not everybody who is cut out for a soldier's life.

cut through **atajar:** He cut through the forest in order to save time.
cortar (de un lado a otro): The dressmaker cut through the cloth.

cut under **refugiarse (debajo de algún sitio):** The rabbit cut under the hedge when it saw the eagle.

cut up **cortar (en pedacitos):** The housewife cut the onion up in pieces.
criticar: The critics really cut up his latest book.
cortar (en jirones): The boy cut the newspaper up in strips.
meterse por un lugar (para despistar): He cut up a side road to avoid the police block.
afectar: The news of his friend's death really cut him up.
destruir: The attacking forces cut the defenders up completely.

D

dance about **moverse de un lado a otro:** The child danced about waiting for the door to be opened.

dance away **continuar bailando:** They danced the whole night away.

dance to **bailar al son de (música):** I like dancing to slow music.

dash at **lanzarse contra:** A big dog dashed at our cat in the street, but the cat escaped.

dash away **echar a un lado (de un empujón):** The drunkard dashed the imploring woman away angrily and went into the pub.

dash back **regresar corriendo:** Freddy dashed back home from school in order to get his sandwiches.

dash down **bajar corriendo:** The young boy dashed down the stairs and shot out without saying goodbye.

dash in **entrar corriendo:** The door opened and two children dashed in.

dash into **entrar corriendo en:** I must dash into this shop for a minute; I forgot to buy butter.

dash off **salir corriendo:** He dashed off as if there were a mad dog at his heels.
escribir muy deprisa: She dashed off a letter and hurried out to catch the next post.
hacer algo apresuradamente: You should take a little more care and not dash things off like that.

dash out **salir corriendo:** He said he must dash out and get a newspaper in order to see the news.

dash up **subir corriendo:** By dashing up the steps he was just in time to stop me from falling.

dawn on **empezar a entender:** It suddenly dawned on me that he wanted me to go.

deal in **traficar con:** He was arrested for dealing in smuggled goods.
incluir (a alguien) en un juego de cartas: Sit down at the table, we'll deal you in.
comerciar con: The new shop on the corner deals in toys.

deal out **distribuir (cantidades iguales):** When the men were seated at the table, someone dealt out the cards.

deal with **tratar con:** We never deal with him now since he was sent to prison for theft.
controlar: It is very difficult for a teacher to deal with a class of forty pupils.

die away **desvanecerse (sonidos):** When the thunder died away, the sky cleared once again.

die down **disminuir (un alboroto):** The spectators' annoyance died down according as the match progressed and their team played well.

die off **morir (como moscas):** When the plague reached that city, thousands died off before help came.

die out **extinguirse:** Many species of wild animals and birds are dying out due to pollution and indiscriminate killing.

die over **olvidarse (un hecho):** The rumours of their defeat soon died over and they were ready to begin again.

dig down **ahondar:** The rescuers dug down in the hope of finding the buried miner.

dig in **atrincherarse:** The soldiers dug themselves in.

dig on **seguir cavando:** The foreman told the workers to dig on until the whistle went for tea.

dig out **encontrar:** We finally dug them out where they were hiding.
hacer un hoyo: They dug out a deep hole in the sand.

dig under **socavar:** The motion of the water dug a hollow under the river bank.

dig up **cavar (un terreno por entero):** He digs the garden up every spring.
encontrar: I dug up an interesting book in the second-hand bookshop.
desenterrar: The pirates dug up the buried treasure and took it to their ship.

dine in **cenar en casa:** We usually dine in all the week, but we go to a restaurant on Saturday evening.

dine out **cenar fuera:** The Joneses are dining out tonight with some friends.

do away with **matar:** He did away with his victims by strangling them.
acabar con (un asunto): It is time we did away with this business of paying tributes.
abolir: Capital punishment was done away with by the last government.

do down **engañar:** The salesman did him down and by charging him double the price.

do for **matar:** He threatened to do for me unless I paid him at once.

asistir (hacer de asistenta): She said she did for a gentleman who worked in the City.
ser apropiado: Will this car do for your purpose or do you want a bigger one?
arruinar: The continuous rain and wind did for the corn harvest.

do in **matar:** The neighbours said he had done his mother-in-law in and buried her in the garden.
engañar: Be careful when you buy anything in that market; they often do customers in.
dejar exhausto: That hard work nearly did me in.

do into **traducir a (mencionando el idioma):** His book has been done into several languages.

do out **asear:** This cupboard hasn't been done out for ages.
decorar: The room has been done out so nicely that it looks like a palace.

do over **retocar:** You'll have to do it over in places; the stains are showing through.
decorar: They did the room over quickly, as they wanted to move the furniture in.

do up **atarse (los zapatos):** You do up your shoes after you've put them on, not before!
empaquetar: The parcel was done up in coloured paper.
abrocharse (con botones): He did up his coat before stepping into the street.
restaurar: They did the old house up until it was habitable.
poner en orden: Your things are all over the place; you'll have to do the room up.
volver a decorar: They're doing the house up again.

do with **venirle (algo) bien a alguien:** He said he could do with a second helping as he was very hungry.

do without **pasarse sin:** I'm afraid you'll have to do without the television this weekend; it's broken.

double back **doblar (por la mitad):** If you double the map back, you can read it more easily.
volver (por el mismo sendero): The escaping prisoner doubled back so as to throw his pursuers off the track.

double up **doblarse:** He doubled up in pain when he was hit in the stomach.

drag away **llevarse arrastrando:** The tiger dragged the dead buffalo away into the jungle.

drag down **bajar arrastrando:** The murderer dragged the dead body down the stairs.
arrastrar (a la ruina): The man was a gambler and dragged his family down with him.

drag in **sacar (un tema):** Why do you always have to drag in the subject of women's rights?
meter arrastrando: The fishermen dragged the nets in.

drag into **meter arrastrando en:** She dragged the heavy log into the kitchen.

drag off **llevarse a la fuerza:** The struggling protesters were dragged off to the police vans.

drag on **alargarse innecesariamente:** The talk dragged on until well into the evening.

drag out **sacar arrastrando:** The barman dragged the drunk out of the pub.

drag up **subir arrastrando:** The exhausted fugitive dragged himself up to the top of the wall.
arrancar: The hurricane had dragged the tree up by the roots.

draw away **alejarse:** The boat drew slowly away from the pier.

draw back **descorrer (una cortina):** The woman drew back the edge of the curtain when she heard the argument in the street.

draw back from **retroceder:** The crowd drew back from the edge of the platform when the train came in.
mantenerse alejado de: The shy girl drew back from the rest of the people at Tom's party.
retractarse, volverse atrás (en el último momento): He will lie readily but will draw back from perjury.

draw down **provocar:** Such actions can only draw down the anger of heaven.
bajar (una persiana): Draw the blind down; night is approaching.

draw in **economizar:** You should draw in a little instead of spending so much.
aspirar (aire): He drew in a deep breath and dived into the river.
acortarse (los días): It is autumn; the days are drawing in little by little.
dibujar: He sketched a house and drew in rooms and a stairs.
atraer: The advertisement I put in the paper drew in a lot of people.
meter: A cat draws in its claws when it is playing.
entrar (un tren en la estación): The train drew slowly into the station.

draw off **retirarse:** The wolves drew off when they heard the voices of the hunters.
quitarse (una prenda): She drew off her gloves and placed them on the table.

draw on **recurrir a:** In the criticism of Eliot he draws heavily on people like Leavis.
ponerse (una prenda): The woman drew on her gloves and took up her handbag.
acercarse: The boat drew on until it was within hailing distance of the ship.
retirar (fondos): As he was hard up, he had to draw on his savings.

draw out **sacar:** When I saw him furtively drawing a gun out of his pocket, I realized his intentions.
alargarse (los días): The days are drawing out now that it is spring.
estirar: He drew a tape measure out and measured the windows.
sonsacar: With a great deal of cunning he managed to draw out their secret.
extraer: The hunter drew the arrow out of the animal before skinning it.
prolongar: The chairman drew his speech out until everybody was bored.
sacar (fondos): I've just been to the bank to draw out the last of my savings.
salir (un tren de la estación): The train drew slowly out of the station and gradually gathered speed.
hacer hablar: He's very good at telling jokes if you can only draw him out.

draw over **hacer cambiar de opinión:** They drew him over to their side by the force of their argument.

draw round **rodear:** The students drew round the teacher attentively while he began the experiment.
agruparse: They all drew round to listen to the speaker.

draw up **estirarse:** The little man drew himself up to his full height and gave his opinion.
redactar, preparar (un documento): The government is drawing up a plan to combat inflation and unemployment.
detenerse (yendo en vehículo o a caballo): The horseman drew up at the door of the inn and called loudly for ale.
formar (las tropas): The two armies drew up facing each other on opposite sides of the river.
sacar (de un pozo): You have to turn this handle in order to draw the bucket up.
hacer (una lista): I want you to draw up a list of all the things we need for the party.
alinearse: The runners were drawn up at the starting line waiting for the signal.

dream up **imaginar:** He's always dreaming up fantastic plans for getting rich overnight.

dress down **echar una bronca:** You should have heard the boss dressing them down.

dress up **vestirse elegantemente:** There he goes to meet his girl, all dressed up in his best clothes!
disfrazarse: Terence dressed up as Napoleon for the party and his wife dressed up as Cleopatra.

drink away **beber (despreocupadamente):** We saw him drinking away in a pub with a group of his mates.

drink down **beber (de un trago):** She drank down the medicine with a grimace and then popped a sweet into her mouth.

drink in **aspirar (el aire):** He stood on the hill top and drank in the fresh morning air.
absorber (mentalmente y con interés): The old man drank the news in greedily.

drink out of **beber (de una taza, vaso):** We drink tea out of a teacup.

drink to **brindar, beber (a la salud de):** The guests drank to the health of the happy couple.

drink up **apurar (beberse todo):** The host invited his guests to drink up and have some more.

drive about **ir en coche (de acá para allá):** They were driving about for an hour before they found a hotel.

drive at **insinuar:** We knew what he was driving at when he said he was broke.
dirigir hacia: The witness said he only drove the car at the man to frighten him.
golpear: He drove at his assailant with a right-hand blow that left him stunned.

drive away **ahuyentar:** The man drove the barking dogs away with a stick.
marcharse (en coche): He drove away from the scene of the accident without reporting it to the police.

drive back **rechazar (hacer retroceder):** He drove the other man back with a hard blow to the face.
regresar (en coche): We are driving back home the day after tomorrow.

drive by **pasar (en coche):** He saw me but he didn't stop. He just drove by.

drive in **meter (a golpes):** The carpenter drove the nail in with a hammer.
entrar (conduciendo): He opened the door of the garage and drove in.

drive into **entrar en (conduciendo):** He drove into the garage and switched off the engine.
meter en (a golpes): The farmer drove the cow into the stall with blows of his stick.
chocar contra: The drunken driver drove into a tree and was injured.

drive off **marcharse (en coche):** They said goodbye and drove off on their honeymoon.
ahuyentar: He managed to drive the hyena off with a burning stick.

drive on **seguir conduciendo:** He saw me waving but he drove on without stopping.

drive out **salir (en coche):** Mr and Mrs Parker drove out to spend the day in the country.
expulsar: After many years of fighting, they drove the enemy out of the country.

drive over **ir de visita (en coche):** We are planning to drive over and see you one of these days.

pasar (nubes): A fleet of clouds drove over the sky.
arrollar (adrede): The tank drove over the barrier without stopping.

drive to **ir a (en coche):** We are driving to the dance on Sunday if you'd like to come.
obligar (a alguien a hacer algo): She complained that her husband drove her to drink.

drive up **llegar (en coche):** When we drove up we saw a group of people talking excitedly.

drive up to **llegar hasta (en coche):** He drove up to the front door and got out of the car.

drop away **disminuir:** Attendance at our meetings has dropped away a lot in the past few months.

drop back **quedarse rezagado:** Kenneth Brown dropped back to speak to me.

drop down **dejar caer:** The boy dropped the stone down the well.
dejarse caer: He dropped down into the armchair with a sigh of content.
caerse: The wind caused the fruit to drop down.

drop in **visitar (sin anunciarse):** The Joneses dropped in as we were about to have tea.

drop into **dejar caer en (dentro):** He dropped a penny into the poor man's hat.
dejarse caer en: The old man dropped into a chair and mopped his face.
caer en (una mala costumbre): Poor John, he's dropped into bad ways.

drop off **disminuir:** Attendance at lectures has dropped off considerably this term.

caerse (desprenderse): The leaves drop off the trees in autumn.
quedarse dormido: She dropped off to sleep while she was watching television.
dejar bajar (a alguien de un vehículo): Drop me off at the next corner, please.

drop on **caer sobre:** The apple dropped on the boy's head as he was passing under the tree.

drop out **dejar de asistir:** He dropped out of the course and started looking for a job.
caerse (el pelo, un diente): One of his teeth dropped out as he was eating.
desaparecer: She dropped completely out of their lives after they were married.
darse de baja: He dropped out of the team because of ill health.

dry up **secarse totalmente:** Keep the stain moist; if it dries up, it will be hard to remove later.
quedarse sin palabras: He began talking but dried up after a few minutes.

dust off **quitar el polvo (de un objeto):** The librarian dusted off the old dictionary and handed it to the student.

dust out **limpiar el polvo (de un lugar):** I found this old newspaper while I was dusting out my room this morning.

dwell on **extenderse sobre (un tema hablando mucho):** You dwelled too much on the theme of public generosity and embarrassed the wealthier members of your audience.

E

ease away **aflojar:** The men eased the rope away and the load fell to the ground.

ease off **aliviarse:** The pain eased off after he took the medicine.
reducir (la tensión): The tension eased off considerably when the speaker made some jokes.
amainar: I'm sure the rain will ease off before noon.
levantar poco a poco (una tapa): You should use this screw to ease the lid off.

ease up **aflojar:** The pressure eased up considerably under the new governor.

eat away **seguir comiendo:** He ate away until there was nothing left on the plate.
corroer: Part of the rock was eaten away by the action of the salt water.
roer: The upholstery was eaten away by vermin.

eat in **comer en casa:** We don't go to the restaurant often; we eat in.

eat into **corroer:** The acid ate into the metal.

eat off **comer en:** My uncle is so rich that he always eats his meals off silver plates.

eat out **comer fuera de casa:** Don't come to visit us tonight; we're eating out.

eat up **comerse todo:** The hungry boy ate up all the rice pudding.
consumirse (de envidia): She was eaten up with envy at her sister's good luck.

empty into **verter en:** Now empty the milk into the bowl.

desembocar en: The Amazon empties into the Atlantic Ocean.

empty out **vaciar:** He empties his pockets out every night before he goes to bed.

end in **terminar en (un extremo):** This rope ends in a knot.
terminar en (un estado): Tim says that Jack's plan will end in failure.

end off **concluir:** The professor ended off his lecture with some amusing stories.

end up **acabar:** After the party I ended up with a headache.
Ir a parar: Where shall we end up with all this drug problem?

enter in **anotar una entrada en (un libro):** The cashier entered the day's takings in a book.

enter on **emprender:** At the age of sixty he entered on the greatest undertaking of his life: marriage.

enter up **anotar (en un libro):** He entered the lists up and totalled them.

even up **igualar:** Take a seat at that table to even up the groups.

explain away **explicar satisfactoriamente:** Your fingerprints are on the gun and there are bloodstains on your clothes; how can you explain that away?

F

face about **volver la mirada:** She faced about and let out a nerve-shattering yell.
dar media vuelta: The two antagonists faced about and prepared to fight.

face away **apartar (la mirada):** The teacher knew the girl was lying because she faced away when he was talking to her.

face down **derrotar (con valentía):** The new chairman faced his opponent down.

face round **girar la cara:** Now face round and I'll cut your hair at the back.

face up **encararse:** He faced up to the difficult situation with courage.

fade away **debilitarse gradualmente (una intención, un sonido, un color):** Betty says that her brother's enthusiasm for running will soon fade away.
desaparecer: All resistance faded away before the new onslaught.

fade down **reducir el sonido gradualmente:** He faded the music down because the children were asleep.

fade off **desvanecerse (sonidos):** The noise faded off into the distance.

fade out **fundirse (imágenes):** The film faded out on a scene of the horseman riding away.

fade up **subir el sonido gradualmente:** He faded the music up once the children were awake again.

fall across **encontrar (por casualidad):** I'd been looking for it for a long time till I fell across it by chance.

fall away **debilitarse:** Resistance gradually fell away.
disminuir (en número): Attendance at classes has fallen away considerably.
abandonar (desertar): His followers fell away when he began to preach violence.
hacer cuesta (el terreno): From here the ground falls away gently to the river.
desviarse de: What a lot of people fall away from the right path in life!

fall back **replegarse (las tropas):** The troops fell back in order as far as the fortifications.

fall back on **recurrir a:** The irate parent fell back on threats when persuasion failed.
refugiarse en: The small country fell back on the protection of its powerful neighbour.

fall down **caerse:** The picture was badly hung and fell down the next day.
postrarse: She fell down before her wronged husband and begged forgiveness.

fall for **dejarse engañar por:** Fancy a smart man like you falling for a simple trick like that!
ser atraído por: She looked so helpless and appealing that he could not help falling for her.

fall from **caerse de:** The leaves fall from the trees in autumn.

fall in **caerse (a un pozo, río):** When he looked down into the well he saw that the cat had fallen in.
hundirse (venirse abajo): The roof of the house fell in an hour ago.
terminar: When does the lease on your shop fall in?
formar (las tropas): The commanding officer ordered the troops to fall in.

fall in with **encontrarse con:** Who do you think I fell in with but old John!
estar de acuerdo con: I wish you would fall in with my views.

fall into **iniciar (una conversación):** As soon as they met, they fell into conversation.
incluir (en una categoría): Sycamores fall into the category of deciduous trees.
formar cola: The children fell into line in front of the ice cream bar.
acostumbrarse: He fell into the habit of going for a long walk every morning.
caerse a (un río, pozo): The boy fell into the river and ruined his clothes.

fall off **disminuir (en número):** The number of students attending class has fallen off.
desprenderse: A brick fell off the top of the wall and killed the cat.
retirarse: The marauding band fell off and regrouped for another attack.
desertar (de un partido): His supporters soon fell off when he started to talk nonsense.
perderse (una costumbre): It seems that that custom has fallen off lately.
menguar: Their zeal soon fell off and they lost interest.
declinar: Their enthusiasm waned and fell off due to internal bickering.
decaer: The quality of the firm's products fell off and sales consequently dropped.
pasar de moda: The use of voluminous undergarments fell off long before our epoch.

fall on **caer sobre (atacar):** They fell on the enemy and routed them.
advertir (por casualidad): My eye fell on a curious passage in this novel.

fall out **suceder:** As it fell out we didn't need the car after all.

romper (las amistades): They fell out over a trifle.
romper filas (las tropas): The officer ordered the men to fall out.
caerse (de dentro afuera): When he lifted the bag a coin fell out.

fall out of **caer (en desuso):** Curling irons fell out of use long ago.
caerse de (un bolsillo, una ventana): A coin fell out of my pocket as I was coming home.

fall over **tropezar y caerse:** Have you ever heard of anyone falling over a matchstick?
despeñarse: He fell over the cliff edge and into the sea.

fall through **fracasar:** Negotiations fell through and the strike continued.
caerse (atravesando algo): Be careful when you skate on the thin ice; you may fall through.

fall to **ponerse a (hacer algo con ahinco):** The gang fell to with a will and finished the job.
tocar (en suerte): It fell to Harold to see the ugly girl out.

fall under **estar comprendido en:** What heading does this sort of crime fall under?
incurrir: He fell under the temptation of robbing the bank.
caer debajo de: The poor man fell under the bus and was killed.

fan out **desplegarse (en abanico):** The police fanned out to catch all the protesters in the demonstration.
desplegar en abanico (las cartas): The gambler fanned the cards out to see them better.

fasten down **sujetar:** When I went to move the chair I found it was fastened down to the floor.

fasten up **abrocharse:** He fastened up his coat and set out.
atar (asegurar): The yacht was fastened up for the night.

fed up **harto:** We are all fed up when we have too much work.

feed into **introducir datos (en una máquina):** The data was fed into the computer by the secretary.

feed up **sobrealimentar:** The housewife fed the turkey up so that it would be fat for Christmas.

feel about **buscar palpando:** He felt about on the table for his glasses.

feel down **sentirse deprimido:** Wet dark days always make me feel down.

feel for **buscar palpando:** The frightened child felt for her mother's hand.
compadecerse de: I really felt for him when he lost his job.

feel on **opinar sobre:** How do you feel on the latest craze of the young?

feel out **sentirse aislado:** Shy people always feel out at parties when the others are talking.

fence off **vallar:** The Browns have fenced their garden off to keep dogs out.

fence out **separar (con una valla):** They did so to fence out the neighbour's goat.

fetch out **sacar (algo que estaba almacenado):** As the weather is warm, it's time to fetch out the garden chairs.

fight back **defenderse:** Even a rat will fight back when it is cornered.

fight down **dominar:** The firemen fought the flames down eventually.
sobreponerse a: He had to fight down a feeling of nausea when he saw the accident.

fight for **luchar por:** Many people all over the world fight for justice.

fight into **abrirse camino (a base de golpes):** He fought into the crowd to rescue his family.

fight off **repeler (un ataque):** Tired as they were, the garrison fought off attack after attack.

fight on **seguir luchando:** The two men fought on until they were covered with blood.

fight out **luchar hasta el final:** The brave boxer fought it out to the bitter end.

fight through **luchar (hasta que se alcanza un resultado):** The stricken man fought through and conquered his illness.

figure on **contar con, proyectar:** We'd figured on your brother helping us.

figure out **descifrar:** I couldn't figure out what he had written.
comprender: I just can't figure her out!
resolver (un problema): We still haven't figured out how to do it.

file down **limar:** The carpenter filed the protruding nail point down.

file off **marcharse desfilando:** They filed off round the corner and were lost to sight.

fill in **rellenar (un hueco):** The carpenter filled in the holes with putty.
rellenar (un formulario): Can you help me to fill in my tax form?

fill out **rellenar (un formulario):** When he had filled out the questionnaire he heaved a sigh of relief.
crecer (hacerse grande): Not only has he got big, but he has also filled out a lot.

fill up **llenar (un formulario):** Fill up this form and hand it in to Miss Smith.
rellenar: The bricklayer filled up the cracks with cement.
llenar totalmente: The host filled up our glasses and put on a record.

find out **averiguar:** Can you find out when the bus leaves?
sorprender (en un acto delictivo): Charles Jones was found out cheating in the exam.

finish off **completar:** Dinner was finished off with an enormous slab of cake.
terminar: Do you think you can finish off the remaining work before lunchtime?
rematar: The soldiers finished off the wounded with the butts of their guns.

finish up **terminar (consumir del todo):** Can anyone finish up the rest of this pie?

fire at **disparar sobre:** The farmer fired at the watchful crows but didn't kill any of them.

fire away **disparar (durante largo tiempo):** The heavy artillery fired away deafeningly for twenty minutes.
empezar a preguntar: If you have any questions to ask, fire away!

fire back **contestar al fuego:** They opened fire and we fired back.

fire off **hacer fuego (con un arma):** They fired off their guns in salute when the king arrived.
proferir: The bad-tempered farmer fired off a volley of oaths when the horse trod on his foot.

fire on **seguir disparando:** The commanding officer ordered the men to fire on.

fire up **enfadarse:** When they left the house in a mess she fired up and ordered them out.

fit in **acoplar:** He's just fitted a new gear lever in the car.

fit into **encajar en:** The carpenter fitted the peg into the hole.
caber en: Can another person fit into the lift?

fit on **acoplar:** The plumber fitted the washer on and then the tap worked perfectly.

fit out **equipar:** Fitted out with the latest climbing gear, the mountaineers set out.
armar: The modern army needs to be fitted out with modern equipment.

fit up **equipar:** The kitchen was fitted up with the latest gadgets.

fix up **reparar:** He soon fixed up the broken toys for his son.
organizar: I hear they are fixing up something special.

flame out **arder:** The petrol-soaked heap of clothes flamed out when he put a match to it.

flame up **enfurecerse:** She flamed up when she was accused of shoplifting.

flare up **estallar en llamas:** Bonfires flared up all over the city.
enfurecerse: The man flared up when the children's ball hit him.

flash up **sostener algo en alto:** The news of the team's success was flashed up on a giant screen.

fling away **arrojar lejos:** He flung the letter away without reading it.

fling down **arrojar al suelo:** The boy flung down the rodent he had caught.

fling off **arrojar:** Jim flung off his hat and whooped with joy.
romper (las amistades): Don't fling off old friends before acquiring new ones.

fling out **extender (los brazos):** Mrs Jones flung her arms out and caught her little nephew.

fling up **darse por vencido:** He flung it up after trying it for the umpteenth time.
abandonar: I heard he flung up his job and went to Australia.

flood out **inundar (totalmente):** Last week the rain flooded out our garage.

flow into **desembocar en:** The river Ebro flows into the Mediterranean Sea.

flow out **brotar:** His blood flowed out and reddened the ground.

flow over **rebosar:** The glass flowed over when he emptied the bottle into it.

fly about **volar de acá para allá:** Bats were flying about in the half light.

fly at **abalanzarse sobre:** The fierce dog flew at the burglar.

fly away **escapar volando:** We used to have a bird in the cage but it flew away.

fly back **volver deprisa:** I must fly back to the office; the boss doesn't know I'm out.

fly down **bajar volando:** A bird flew down from the tree and picked at the crumbs.

fly in **entrar apresuradamente:** She threw open the door and flew in as if she were pursued by a bull.

fly off **salir despedido:** While I was driving the nail in, the head of the hammer flew off.
salir volando: The instant I stepped out into the garden all the sparrows flew off.

fly on **seguir volando:** Wild geese can fly on for miles without seeming to get tired.

fly out **salir corriendo:** She flew out of the office and across the street to the sandwich bar.

fly over **volar sobre:** We live near the airport, so planes are continually flying over our house.

fly up **subir volando:** The bird flew up and perched on the top of the tree.

fly upon **abalanzarse sobre:** She flew upon him brandishing a roller and screaming.

fold over **doblar:** The salesman folded over the page in the wallpaper pattern book.

fold up **doblar (para guardar):** He folded his handkerchief up and put it into his coat pocket.

follow in **seguir (a alguien) hacia adentro:** I don't know whose the dog is; it followed me in when I opened the door.

follow on **resultar (como consecuencia):** This follows on from what we said about punctuality.
acudir (más tarde): You can go ahead: I'll follow on in a few minutes.

follow out **seguir (instrucciones):** Although I followed out all the instructions carefully, I couldn't get the machine to work.
seguir (un consejo, instrucciones): I want my instructions to be followed out.

follow through **seguir (hasta el final), investigar:** He followed his quest through to the end.

follow up **seguir de cerca:** We've been following up your progress in the news reports.
profundizar, investigar: The idea sounded interesting and I decided to follow it up.

fool about **hacer el tonto:** Stop fooling about and get on with your work!

fool away **malgastar:** He fooled away not only his time but his fortune.

force back **hacer retroceder:** The boxer's attack forced his opponent back into the corner.

force into **obligar (a alguien) a hacer algo:** He was forced into resigning.
meter a la fuerza: Don't force the key into the lock; it may break.

freeze up **helarse totalmente:** The kitchen window is frozen up and I can't open it.

G

gamble away **perder en el juego:** He gambled away all his fortune in one week.

gather in **recolectar y guardar (la cosecha):** We'll rest when the crop is gathered in.

gather up **recoger (lo que está desperdigado):** She gathered up the broken pieces and put them in the dustbin.

get about **ir de un lado para otro:** The old man gets about all right with the help of a stick.
difundirse (las noticias): The news got about that he was already married.
estar levantado (después de una enfermedad): The doctor told him that he would be able to get up and about in a week.
ponerse a trabajar: When the boss came in, he ordered the chattering typists to get about their work.

get across **cruzar:** It is difficult to get across this street in the rush hours.
hacer entender: After many efforts I finally got it across to him that he should see a specialist.

get along **ir tirando:** The old man said he was getting along all right apart from some trouble.
conseguir (avanzar): See if you can get along as far as the corner without help.
progresar: The business is getting along very well.

get along with **arreglárselas con:** You'll have to get along with the old car if you can't afford to buy a new one.
marcharse: Get along with you this moment; I don't want to hear another word from you!
soportar a: I can't get along with that sister of hers.
congeniar con: He gets along well with his in-laws.

get around **ir de un sitio para otro:** He gets around a lot on his little motorbike.
divulgarse (las noticias): The news got around that there was going to be a takeover.

get at **alcanzar:** Put the food where the cat can't get at it.
insinuar: I can't quite understand what you're getting at.
burlarse de: They are always getting at him about his stormy love affairs.
ponerse a (hacer algo): You have a lot of work to do, so get at it!

get away **escaparse:** The butterfly got away when the boy opened his hand.
tomarse vacaciones, librarse de las obligaciones diarias: Let's see if we can get away for the weekend.

get away from **escaparse de:** With a flick of its tail the fish got away from the boy's groping fingers.
alejarse de: Wouldn't you like to get away from these depressing slums?

get away with **escaparse con:** The robbers held up the pay delivery van and got away with a million.

get away with it **salirse con la suya:** If you think you can get away with it, you're wrong.

get back **regresar:** My parents leave tomorrow and get back on the 30th.
recuperar: I heard that Sir Joshua Grimes got back the paintings that were stolen.
retirarse, apartarse (de un peligro): "Get back!" shouted the policeman: "The building is collapsing!"

get by **sortear (obstáculos):** A cool head can help you to get by in a lot of difficult situations.
pasar (dar por bueno): Your work is not very good, but it will get by.

get down **bajar:** He got the suitcases down from the rack and had them ready.
bajarse, apearse: The weary travellers got down and stretched their legs.
deprimir: This cold wet weather gets me down.
descolgar: Can you get that picture down from there?

get down to **ponerse a (hacer algo):** You'll have to get down to it if you want to finish today.

get in **entrar:** Get in, it's too cold to stand here outside.
meter: The donkey got its head in through the fence but it couldn't withdraw it.
ganar (en unas elecciones): After a brilliant campaign the workers' party got in.
subir (a un vehículo): They got in and drove off.
volver (a casa): Dad doesn't get in until nine o'clock.
llegar (un tren): The train gets in at half-past seven.

get in with **hacer amistad con:** He got in with bad company and got into trouble.

get into **entrar en (mencionando el lugar):** The driver told the passengers to get into the vehicle.
ponerse (una prenda): She got into the dress and stood in front of the mirror.
familiarizarse con (algo): You'll find it's not so difficult once you get into it.

get off **apearse:** When the bus stopped, we got off with our cases.
partir (en una carrera): With a roar of engines the cars got off from the starting line.
quedarse dormido: He couldn't get off to sleep until after midnight.

bajarse de: The man got off the horse and tied the reins to the fence.
salir (de viaje): They got off pretty early on their way to the beach.
tomarse un tiempo libre: He got a day off from work when his wife had a baby.
quitar (de una superficie): We got the graffiti off the wall by using steam.
quitarse (una prenda): When she got her shoes off, she massaged her toes.
quitarse (de un sitio): Get off that chair and let Mrs Green sit down.
despachar (enviar): Try and get these letters off by the first post.
salir absuelto: I believe he was accused of a crime once but got off.

get on **subir (a un autobús):** They told me to get on the number nineteen bus and to get off at Marble Arch.
ponerse (una prenda): The farmer got his wellington boots on by pulling hard.
congeniar: The two couples get on quite well together.
montar: He got on his horse and rode away into the sunset.
hacerse mayor: He was getting on in years and could no longer be called young.

get on for **aproximarse a (una edad, una hora):** She must have been getting on for thirty when she married.

get onto **subirse a:** He got onto the roof by climbing through a skylight.

get on with **seguir con (una tarea):** Get on with what you're doing and don't stop to talk.
congeniar con: How are you getting on with your new neighbours?
progresar: I asked her how she was getting on with her new book.

get out **sacar:** He got out a knife and began examining its edge.
publicar: When are they getting your new book out?

apearse: Most of these passengers will be getting out at the next station – Victoria.
quitar (una mancha): That stain can be got out with this liquid.

get out of **salir de:** By the time we got out of the house the moon was high.
quitar de: Get that chair out of my way; I can't walk here!
escaparse de: Few prisoners manage to get out of that prison.
sacar de: He got four people out of the burning house before a beam fell on him.
marcharse de: Once we got out of that town, we swore we'd never return.

get over **acabar con:** I'll be glad to get the interview over.
saltar por encima de: The thief got over the garden wall by vaulting.
restablecerse de (una enfermedad): I heard he had a heart attack; do you know if he got over it?
hacer entender: Did he get his meaning over to the crowd?
superar: I don't know how we're going to get over this difficulty.
ir a: Can you get over to Mary's and telephone from there?

get round **rodear:** The attackers got round the fortification and attacked it from the rear.
divulgarse (una noticia): Word got round that the house was going to be sold.
manejar (a alguien): Don't think you'll get round me like that!
persuadir: The children got round their parents to let them go to the zoo.

get through **pasar por:** I'm afraid we can't get the table through this narrow entrance.
atravesar: He got through the dark silent town without any difficulty.
aprobar (un examen): He got through his finals not without some difficulty.

sobrevivir: I don't know how we're going to get through this cold winter.
lograr comunicar por teléfono: She tried to phone them, but she couldn't get through.
llevar a cabo: The party tried hard to get the project through but without success.
convencer: Somehow or other the idea just doesn't get through to me.

get through with **terminar con:** When he got through with the chocolates, he started on the cakes.

get to **llegar a:** When they got to the frontier, they were stopped by an armed guard.
ponerse a (trabajar): The foreman ordered the men to get to work at once.

get under **meterse debajo de:** The animal got under the fence by burrowing.

get up **subirse:** The climber got up the rock face with great difficulty.
levantarse (de la cama): At what time do you get up in the morning?
aumentar (el viento): The wild wind got up to hurricane force and roared through the trees.
organizar: We are getting up a party to celebrate Mary's birthday.
disfrazarse: They got themselves up as Anthony and Cleopatra for the party.
ponerse de pie: He got up when the stranger entered the room.
preparar rápidamente: Can you get up a light lunch before we set off?

get up to **poder acercarse (a alguien):** When I got up to the girl, I could see that she was my neighbour Betty Brown.
tramar algo: The children are all whispering in the corner, but I can't see what they are getting up to.

give away **dar (en matrimonio):** The bride was given away by her father.
regalar: She gave her son's toys away to his poor cousins.
descubrir (un secreto): The plot was given away by the girlfriend of one of the conspirators.
repartir: Any unsold samples are given away free after the exhibition.
echar a perder (una oportunidad): He gave away his chance of being elected when he appeared drunk on TV.

give back **devolver:** The police gave the bicycle back to its owner.
retroceder (echarse hacia atrás): Give back there; the train is coming now!

give in **acceder:** His arguments convinced me, so I gave in and signed the document.
darse por vencido: They kept on fighting as neither wanted to give in.
entregar: The teacher told us to give our exams in.

give off **despedir (olor):** The rotting vegetation gave off a disagreeable smell.

give out **acabarse:** The supply of drink gave out before the party finished.
distribuir: Hymn books were given out at the church door.
anunciar: It was given out that the firm was bankrupt.
despedir (olor): The boiling pitch gave out a strong smell.
averiarse: The car gave out before they reached the town.

give over **perder (la esperanza):** When all hope was given over, the unexpected happened.
desistir, dejar (de hacer algo): He gave over in his attempts to convince her to marry him.
entregar: The prisoner was given over to the police.
cesar (la lluvia): The rain gave over and the sun came out.
darse a (un vicio): He gave himself over to vice and evil ways.

give round **pasar (la comida en la mesa compartiéndola):** My sister give the food round to everyone when we were sitting at the table.

give up **renunciar:** The mountaineers gave up climbing through weariness.
darse por vencido: I give up; I don't know the answer to the riddle.
dejar (una relación de amistad): His girlfriend has given him up.
dejar (un vicio): The doctor told him to give up smoking and drinking.
dejar (un cargo): He had to give up his welfare work when he took up politics.
abandonar (una idea): It was a long time before people gave up believing that the earth was flat.
dejar (una costumbre): Many people have given up wearing hats.

give up to **rendirse a:** The wanted man gave himself up to the police.
ceder: Give your seat up to this old lady.

give upon **dar (una ventana a un lugar):** The rear windows give upon the river and the wood beyond.

glue down **pegar (con cola):** You should glue the mat down at the edges so that it won't curl.

go about **ocuparse de:** She told him coldly to go about his business.
ir (de un lado para otro): He went about like a drunken man.
empezar (el trabajo): The foreman told them to go about their work.
difundirse: When the news went about, nobody believed it at first.
ponerse a (hacer algo): You must go about mending that leaking pipe.

go across **atravesar:** He went across the field and into the thicket.

go after **ir tras:** The dog went after the sheep running and barking.

go along **continuar:** Go along to the next traffic lights and turn left.
ir (a lo largo de): It's nice to go along the river on an evening in May.
ir (a algún sitio cerca): Go along to the shop and buy a packet of salt.

go along with **estar de acuerdo con:** I go along with most of what he said.
acompañar a: He went along with her as far as her house.

go at **acometer:** She went at the burglar with a carving knife.
ponerse a: They went at their work with enthusiasm.

go away **marcharse:** She told him to go away and never to come back.
desaparecer: The pain in his back went away after the doctor's treatment.
alejarse: As he was going away, I noticed that he limped slightly.

go away with **llevarse:** The guest went away with the towels of the hotel.

go back **regresar:** I'll never go back there after what happened.
retroceder: The player went back a few steps to get a good kick at the ball.

go back on **no cumplir la palabra dada:** You can't believe him, he always goes back on his word.

go by **pasar por (un lugar):** As he went by the old homestead he felt sad.
ser conocido por (un nombre): He goes by the name of "Tubby."
regirse por: He always goes by the rules.
ir por (vía): I prefer going by air as it's quicker and more comfortable.
pasar (el tiempo): The years go by and things don't change.

go down **bajar:** The boy went down the stairs two at a time.
sucumbir: The defence went down before the enemy's attack.

hundirse: The ship went down with all hands on board.
ponerse (el sol): As the sun was going down it started to rain.
ser recibido: The new President's speech went down well.
pasar a (la posteridad): He will go down in the history books as a magnificent failure.
ir por (la calle): As I was going down the street I met Jill.
bajar (el precio): When the market is glutted, prices go down.
dejar (la universidad): When he went down from Oxford he began working in his father's firm.
bajar (de categoría): I hope our team doesn't go down to the Second Division.
ir (de la ciudad al campo): I'm thinking of going down to the country for a few days.

go down in **suspender (un examen):** He went down in Latin.

go down with **caer enfermo con:** He went down with pneumonia and was sent to hospital.

go for **ir por:** Go for a doctor, quickly.
atacar: The woman went for her assailant with an umbrella.
alcanzar (un precio): The house went for ten thousand pounds.

go in **entrar:** Go in and ask the man to move his car.
caber: My car boot is rather small; I doubt if that suitcase will go in.

go in for **entrar (en una competición):** He went in for the half mile, as this was his best distance.
practicar (un deporte): At school he went in for rugby.
dedicarse a: Now he goes in for coin collecting in a big way.

go in with **asociarse con:** I don't want him to go in with that crowd.

go into **entrar en:** He went into the house and shut the door.
caber en: I didn't believe all the objects would go into the bag.
investigar: The police inspector went pretty thoroughly into his past life.

go off **marcharse:** He went off without saying goodbye.
quedarse dormido: Has the baby gone off to sleep yet?
estropearse (alimentos): The food went off because we didn't put it in the fridge.
resultar: Did the show go off as you expected it would?
estallar: The bomb went off and injured four persons.
venderse bien (un producto): The product went off well thanks to a new advertising campaign.
descarrilar: The train went off the rails and turned over.
deteriorarse: The quality of the classes has gone off under the new professor.
pararse (un dolor): The pain went off when she started taking the medicine.
dispararse (un arma): Loaded guns have a habit of going off.
sonar (un timbre): The alarm went off at six o'clock.

go on **continuar:** He went on working after the others had left.
entrar (en escena): He went on the stage dressed as an admiral.
suceder: There's a fight going on down the street.
basarse: I'm simply going on what I was told.
comportarse: If you go on like a clown, don't blame people for laughing.
hablar con enfado: Don't go on like that about such a simple matter.
indicando incredulidad: As he was telling the story there were various exclamations of "go on!"

go on at **regañar:** She went on at her husband for forgetting their anniversary.

go on with **continuar con:** Go on with what you're doing and let me know when you finish.

go out **salir:** Are you going out tonight or do you prefer to stay at home?
pasar de moda: The "crew cut" went out of fashion years ago.

apagarse: The fire went out because there was no fuel.
emigrar: He went out to Australia with his family.
ponerse en huelga: The workers went out on strike for better working conditions.
retroceder (la marea): The mussel pickers went along the beach after the tide had gone out.

go over **examinar:** We went over several houses before deciding on this one.
repasar: You'll need to go over your notes again before the exam.
retocar: You'll have to go over the paintwork a second time.
inspeccionar: They went over the list of candidates and chose the first three.
cambiar (de partido): Old Jones went over to the workers' party.
cruzar: When he had gone over the river he sat down to smoke.
saltar por encima de (accidentalmente): The car went over the cliff into the sea.
ir a: Go over to Smith's and ask for a packet of tea.

go round **hacer una visita:** Go round and see how old Mrs Green is keeping.
ser suficiente: The money will just go round.
dar un rodeo: If you go round by the church you'll take longer.

go through **atravesar (penetrar):** A high-velocity bullet can go through a brick wall.
atravesar (cruzar): You will go through Paris on your way.
sufrir: That country has gone through too many wars.
examinar: I want to go through this thoroughly.
repasar: Can you go through this letter and check it for mistakes?
cumplirse: Everything went through as he had hoped.
dilapidar: They went through a fortune in a short time.
llevar a cabo: He went through with his plan.

go under **ir por debajo de:** The cat went under the fence and out of the garden.
quebrar (un negocio): The business went under due to bad management.
hundirse (un buque): They say the ship went under with all hands.
ser conocido por (un nombre): He goes under the name of Elias Tucker.

go up **subir:** He put out the lights and went up the stairs.
escalar: The mountaineers went up the side of the mountain.
explotar: The ammunition dump went up with a tremendous "bang".
subir (los precios): Prices always go up at Christmas time.
ser erigido (un edificio): There are new buildings going up all the time.

go up to **elevarse hasta:** The balloon went up to the cloud level in a few minutes.
acercarse a: He went up to her and whispered something.
llegar hasta (un precio): The bidding was lively and the price went up to ten thousand.
entrar en la universidad: I hear your son's gone up to Cambridge.
ir (a la ciudad): My wife's gone up to town to do a bit of shopping.

go with **acompañar:** He wanted to go with her to the cinema.
hacer juego (casar): Yellow shoes don't go with a purple dress.

go without **pasarse sin:** Many children have to go without toys at Christmas.

grind down **moler reduciendo a polvo:** Years ago this mill was used to grind the wheat down into flour.

grind up **moler triturando o reduciendo a polvo:** These big rocks will all be ground up to build the new road.

grow down **colgar (una planta):** Tendrils of ivy grew down along the window sides.
enraizarse (una planta): The roots of giant trees grow down many feet into the ground.

grow into **hacerse (una persona):** She has grown into a beautiful young woman.

grow over **cubrir (una planta):** Grass has grown over the place where the old house stood.

grow up **crecer:** When the trees grow up, we are going to prune them.
hacerse mayor: What are you going to be when you grow up?
trepar por (una planta): Ivy grew up the tree and choked it.

H

hammer away **trabajar asiduamente:** He kept hammering away at it until the job was finished.

hammer in **clavar:** The carpenter hammered the nail in.

hammer into **clavar:** The carpenter hammered the nails into the wood.
inculcar: It was hammered into him that he should be a doctor when he grew up.

hammer out **dar forma a martillazos:** The smith hammered the piece of metal out.

hand down **pasar (de padre a hijo):** The old violin was handed down from father to son.

hand in **entregar (a la autoridad):** We have to hand the essays in before the end of the week.

hand on **pasar (de uno a otro):** Each man took a drink and handed the bottle on to the next.
transmitir: We handed on the information as soon as we had received it.

hand out **repartir:** The teacher handed the books out at the beginning of the class.

hand over **entregar (algo reclamado):** He handed the money over to the police.

hand round **pasar (de uno a otro):** The letter was handed round and each person signed his name.

hang about **quedarse a la espera:** The waiter hung about, evidently expecting a tip.
rezagarse: Don't hang about; the taxi is waiting.

hang around **holgazanear:** He's always hanging around with his hands in his pockets.
rezagarse (esperando): I hung around a bit so as not to catch up with them.

hang back **mantenerse apartado:** He hung back because he didn't want to speak to them.
vacilar: The soldiers hung back when the order was given to advance.

hang on **perseverar:** Don't give up now; hang on for another hour or so.
depender: It all hangs on the boss's decision.
perseguir: The detective hung on the suspect's trail.
no colgar (el teléfono): Hang on a minute, my brother wants a word with you.

hang on to **aferrarse a:** Now that everything else is gone, he has only his religion to hang on to.
conservar: My parents hung on to the farm and made a fortune.
escuchar (con atención): The boys hung on to her every word.

hang out **resistir (hasta el final):** My brother Tom hung out to the bitter end.
colgar (mostrando): The shopkeeper hung out his wares.
frecuentar: He often hangs out at Charly's Chop House.
residir: Do you know where old George hangs out?
durar: The Wilsons stayed in Madrid while their money hung out.
asomarse: She hung out of the window, shouting to her friends in the street.

hang over **estar pendiente:** We've got this problem hanging over since last year.
amenazar: It's like a sword of Damocles hanging over our heads.
proyectarse hacia afuera: The grassy bank hung over the river.

hang round **frecuentar (la compañía de alguien):** He's always hanging round the Smith girl.
frecuentar (un lugar), reunirse alrededor de: John usually hangs round the Railway Café.

hang up **colgar:** Hang my coat up in the wardrobe, please.
demorar: The talks were hung up while the two sides considered the propositions.
colgar (el teléfono): I must hang up now; somebody's knocking at the door.

happen on **encontrarse con.** Who do you think I should happen on but young Jones!

have back **mandar devolver:** We'll have that back if you don't want it.

have in **invitar a alguien a la casa de uno:** I'd like to have Roger and Muriel in for a few drinks.
mandar venir: We shall be having the plumber in next week.

have off **cortar:** In olden times they'd have your head off for a remark like that.
quitarse: He had his coat off and was working in the garden.

have on **llevar puesto:** What did he have on when you saw him?

have out **invitar a alguien a una comida fuera de casa:** We'd like to have you and your wife out for dinner next Sunday.
sacarse (una muela): If your tooth hurts, you'd better have it out.

have over **solucionar:** I'm glad we have that problem over.

have up **mandar subir:** She had me up for a cup of tea and a quiet chat.
llamar a presencia de: We'll have you up before Mr Smith.
llevar a juicio: He was had up in court for dangerous driving.

head in **meter un balón de cabeza:** Wilson scored by heading the ball in.

head off **desviar (para seguir el camino correcto):** The shepherd headed off the flock of sheep.
desviar (una conversación desagradable): When John starts to talk about his illnesses, we try to head him off to another subject.

heap up **hacer un montón:** He heaped food up on the plate.
amasar (una fortuna): He heaped an entire fortune up during the war.

hear about **enterarse de:** Have you heard about my cousin's latest adventure?

hear of **tener noticias de:** He hadn't heard of his brother's arrival when I met him.
tener referencias de: Stilovsky? I've never heard of that artist.

hear out **escuchar hasta el final:** Although he had a lot of work he heard me out.

help away **ayudar (a alguien) a alejarse:** He helped the injured man away from the scene of the accident.

help back **ayudar (a alguien) a volver:** He asked the old lady if he could help her back to her house.
ayudar (a alguien) a recuperar una posición anterior: The old woman fell out of her bed and the nurse helped her back into it.

help down **ayudar (a alguien) a bajar:** The conductor helped the passengers down from the bus.

help in **ayudar (a alguien) a entrar:** The driver held the car door open to help Mrs Benson in.

help into **ayudar (a alguien) a entrar en:** He helped her into the crowded train.

help off with **ayudar (a alguien) a quitarse una prenda:** She helped the child off with his shoes.

help on with **ayudar (a alguien) a ponerse una prenda:** Here, let me help you on with your coat.

help out **ayudar (a alguien) a salir:** He helped the invalid out of the car.
ayudar (a alguien) en una dificultad: Whenever I was in difficulties he always helped me out.

help over **ayudar (a alguien) a pasar por encima de:** He helped her over the stile.
ayudar (a alguien) a pasar una dificultad: He helped me over a difficult period in my life.

help through **ayudar (a alguien) a atravesar una dificultad:** If you can help me through this, I shall be very grateful.

help to **servir:** Let me help you to some more meat.

help up **ayudar (a alguien) a subir:** The climbers helped each other up the mountain side.
ayudar (a alguien) a levantarse: The nurse helped the old man up from the bed.

hem in **cercar:** The village is hemmed in by hills.

hide out **esconderse:** The police found him hiding out in an abandoned farmhouse.

hide up **esconder:** Jack Slater hid up all his money and nobody ever found it.

hire out **alquilar (algo a alguien):** When the farmer finishes his work, he hires his machinery out.

hit off **imitar:** In his imitation of the President he hit him off to perfection.

hit on **dar con:** When the car broke down, we were lucky to hit on a little garage.

hit out **golpear:** When he found himself cornered, he hit out right and left.

hit upon **dar con:** I hope someone hits upon an alternative to petrol.

hold away **mantener alejado:** The boxer held his opponent away with one hand and hit him with the other.

hold back **contener (un ataque):** The ramparts held back the enemy attack.
contenerse (no atreverse): She is a shy girl and always holds back when she is in public.
refrenar: He was able to hold back his anger and so avoided a fight.
vacilar: He held back until it was too late.

hold by **atenerse a:** He is the sort of man who always holds by his principles.

hold down **sujetar:** She held her skirt down with one hand and her hat with the other.
mantener boca abajo: The boy held his opponent down until he submitted.

oprimir: Strong countries always try to hold down their weaker neighbours.
bajar (la cabeza): She held down her head and wept when she heard the news.

hold in **sujetar (caballos, perros):** He had to struggle to hold his horse in as the car roared past.

hold off **aplazar:** I think we can hold the event off until next week.
mantener apartado: She's so popular she has difficulty holding her admirers off.
no llover cuando amenaza: If the rain holds off, we'll go out.

hold on **parar(se):** Hold on a minute, I don't like the tone of your voice!
aguantar: He held on in spite of every difficulty.
continuar: The wind storm held on steadily through the day.
esperar (al teléfono): Hold on a moment, I'll see if Mr Jones is free.

hold onto **agarrarse:** People standing in the tube trains hold onto the straps.

hold out **resistir:** He held out to the bitter end.
ofrecer: I don't think much of the possibilities you hold out.
extender: The beggar held out his hand for money.
durar: Do you think our money will hold out until payday?
ir tirando: I think we can hold out with what we have.

hold over **aplazar, posponer:** The meeting is being held over until next week.
suspender sobre: The cruel boy held the cat over the water.

hold to **aferrarse a (una opinión):** He held to his decision despite his wife's opposition.
mantener (una promesa): Charles is the kind of person who always holds to what he says.

hold up **sostener en alto:** The father held the boy up so that he could see the train.
asaltar (para robar): The bandits held the car up and ordered the driver out.
dificultar: The series of strikes is holding up production.
detener (la marcha): The column was held up while the bridge was repaired.
mantenerse: If the weather holds up, we'll be able to go fishing.

hook up **abrochar:** Can you hook my dress up at the back, please?

hunt down **perseguir:** The bloodthirsty warriors hunted the enemy down.

hunt for **buscar (desesperadamente):** I hunted for it everywhere but couldn't find it.

hunt out **tratar de encontrar:** They were told to hunt him out wherever he was.

hurry along **ir deprisa:** He was hurrying along not looking where he was going
darse prisa: Hurry along, children, or you'll be late for school.

hurry away **salir corriendo:** He hurried away without saying goodbye.

hurry back **regresar corriendo:** Hurry back from the shop; your tea will be ready in a few minutes.

hurry by **pasar deprisa:** The years hurry by as if impatient to be gone.

hurry down **bajar corriendo:** Hurry down, Tom, breakfast's ready!

hurry in **entrar corriendo:** The children hurried in because it was raining.

hurry into **entrar corriendo en:** He hurried into the pub to get a drink before closing time.

hurry off **alejarse deprisa:** He hurried off to meet his girlfriend, his mind happy.

hurry on **seguir deprisa:** The travellers hurried on as they had to reach the inn before nightfall.

hurry out **salir deprisa:** I saw one of the waitresses hurrying out, so I knew they were closing

hurry out of **salir deprisa (de un lugar):** She hurried out of the room on hearing a strange noise outside.

hurry up **darse prisa:** Hurry up, please, it's time!

J

join up **alistarse:** He joined up because he couldn't find work.

jump about **dar saltos:** As it was cold he kept jumping about to get warm.

jump at **abalanzarse sobre:** The dogs jumped at the wounded deer.
aprovechar (una oportunidad): Would you jump at the chance of marrying the boss's daughter?

jump away **apartarse de un salto:** The boxer jumped away as his opponent threw a punch.

jump back **saltar hacia atrás:** He managed to jump back before the wall fell on him.

jump down **saltar desde lo alto:** Many people jumped down from the windows of the burning building.
bajarse de un salto: The speaker jumped down from his box and fled when the police arrived.

jump in **entrar (deprisa en un coche):** Jump in, there's plenty of room in the car.

jump off **apearse de un salto:** It is dangerous to jump off a moving bus or train.

jump on **subirse de un salto:** Robert jumped on the bus as it was about to start.

jump out **salir de un salto:** The parachutists jumped out of the plane.

jump over **saltar por encima:** He jumped over the stream without wetting his feet.
omitir: In his reading he jumped over great chunks he didn't understand.

jump up **sobresaltarse:** Don't jump up every time someone comes into the room!
subir repentinamente: Prices have jumped up spectacularly in the past few weeks.

K

keep at **perseverar:** He kept at it until it was finished.
insistir: She kept at her husband to take her to the theatre.

keep away **impedir acercarse:** The skunk's bad smell keeps its enemies away.

keep away from **mantenerse alejado de:** He's kept away from her since their quarrel.
abstenerse de: He's managed to keep away from drink since his illness.

keep back **apartarse:** The policeman told the people to keep back.
retener: He kept back part of the money, which he never paid.
ocultar (no publicar): I think the newspapers kept back the most important part of the story.
sujetar: The animal was kept back by a rope tied round its neck.
reprimir: She kept back her tears and looked evenly at him.

keep back from **apartarse de:** Bystanders couldn't be kept back from the scene of the accident.

keep by **tener a mano:** It's a good idea to keep a new tin of tea by in case you suddenly need some more.

keep down **someter:** A conquered nation is kept down by its conquerors.
reprimir: He kept down a feeling of anger as he listened.
reducir: The best way to keep expenses down is to spend little.
agacharse: Keep down or you may get hit on the head.

keep in **retener:** The teacher kept the boys in after school.
confinar: The animals are kept in by a fence around the field.
mantener (el fuego): He kept the fire in overnight.

keep off **mantenerse alejado:** He kept himself off and didn't approach the house again.
evitar (un tema): In their discussions they kept off the subject of religion.
no dejar pasar: An umbrella is for keeping the rain off.
rechazar (un ataque): Their stubborn determined defence kept the enemy off.

keep on **seguir (haciendo algo):** The boy kept on talking after the teacher told him to stop.

keep on about **insistir en un tema:** He kept on about the good time he had on holiday last year, boring us to tears.

keep on at **regañar:** She kept on at him about not buying a present for her birthday.

keep out **no dejar entrar:** A high fence around the fort kept the attacking Indians out.
evitar: He kept out all mention of politics in his talk.

keep out of **no entrometerse en:** You should keep out of fights which don't concern you.

keep over **guardar:** Did you keep any drink over from the party?
conservarse: Will this fish keep over the week-end?

keep to **limitarse a:** Keep to non-alcoholic drinks if you're driving.
ajustarse a: If you want to play the game you must keep to the rules.
atenerse a: He is the kind of person who never keeps to what he says.

keep under **sujetar:** A series of edicts were devised to keep the populace under.
dominar: Did the firemen manage to keep the fire under?

keep up **continuar:** The boss told me to keep up the good work and I'd soon get a rise.
mantener (una casa): He's got a house to keep up and a family to look after.
mantener sujeto: The pit roof was kept up by props.
mantener levantado: An aching tooth kept me up all night.

keep up with **mantenerse a nivel de:** Dull students find it difficult to keep up with bright ones.
llevar el mismo paso o velocidad que: The unknown runner kept up with the leaders until the last lap.

kick at **dar una patada a:** The little boy kicked at the ball.

kick away **alejar a patadas:** The man kicked the dog away from the door.

kick back **devolver una patada:** The centre forward kicked back when he was fouled.

kick down **derribar de una patada:** The boy kicked the sandcastles down before the tide came in.

kick in **meter de una patada:** In the last minute, Marlowe kicked the ball in.

kick off **quitarse los zapatos:** He kicked his slippers off and put his feet up, ready for a good nap.
hacer el saque inicial (en el fútbol): The team that lost the toss kicked off.

kick on **seguir dando patadas:** The little boy kicked on until someone opened the door angrily.

kick out **echar de una patada:** The cruel man kicked the poor dog out.

kick out of **echar a patadas de:** The cruel man kicked the poor dog out of the house.
despedir (del trabajo): My friend was kicked out of his job for inefficiency.

kick over **volcar de una patada:** The cow kicked the milking pail over and spilled the milk.

kick up **armar jaleo:** They kicked up a terrible row when they found the mistake out.

kill off **exterminar:** Unscrupulous hunters are killing off many species of animals.

kiss away **calmar a alguien con besos:** Timmy's mother kissed his tears away.

knit up **remendar:** Knit this up if you can!
unirse firmemente (huesos): I heard his broken bone knitted up well.

knock about **maltratar:** They say he knocks his poor wife about a bit.

knock at **llamar a la puerta:** Someone knocked at the door when we were sitting down to dinner.

knock away **retirar de un golpe:** She knocked the swinging curtain rail away.

knock back **beber a grandes tragos:** We managed to knock back fifteen pints of beer in an hour.

knock down **atropellar:** A man was knocked down by a car in our street.
adjudicar (en una subasta): The vase was knocked down to the man who bid highest.
derribar (una casa): They are knocking down all the houses in this street.
rebajar: I wonder if you can knock the price down a bit.
derribar: With one blow the boxer knocked his opponent down.

knock in **derribar (hacia adentro):** They knocked the wall in with sledge hammers.
clavar: The carpenter knocked the nails in with deft blows.

knock into **clavar en:** The carpenter knocked the nails into the wood.

knock off **quitar de un golpe:** The boys' football knocked the old man's hat off.
dejar de trabajar: At what time do you knock off?
descontar (una cantidad): They knock a certain amount off the bill if you pay in cash.
comer rápidamente: The greedy man knocked off a plate of sausages in an instant.
componer rápidamente: He can knock off a poem for you in five minutes.
tirar (hacer caer) por accidente: Sorry! I've knocked the bottle off the table and broken it.

knock on **darse un golpe contra:** As he was entering the shed he knocked his head on a beam.
llamar (a la puerta): He was knocking on the door for a long time before it opened.

knock out **vaciar de un golpe:** He knocked the ash out of his pipe against the wall.
dejar sin sentido: The falling beam knocked him out.

tocar el piano (sin maña): The bar woman knocked out an unharmonious tune on the old piano.
dejar fuera de combate (en el boxeo): Reeves knocked Slevin out in their last fight.

knock over **derribar de un golpe:** The elephant knocked the fence over with its trunk.
afectar: I was absolutely knocked over by the news.
atropellar: She was knocked over by a car as she was crossing the street.

knock up **despertar (llamando a la puerta):** They knocked me up to go fishing with them at six o'clock.
ganar (dinero): He knocked up a good deal of money last year.
hacer improvisadamente: The travellers knocked up a makeshift hut for shelter.
dejar agotado: A half hour's jogging in the morning leaves him knocked up for the day.

L

lace up **atarse (los cordones de los zapatos):** Lace your shoes up or you'll trip over.

last out **aguantar (hasta el final):** Can you last out? It's three miles yet.
durar: I think the patient won't last out till this evening.

laugh at **reírse de:** They were unkindly laughing at the efforts of the fat man to climb the rope.

laugh away **reírse (para disipar preocupaciones):** Those who can laugh away their troubles and griefs are to be envied.
seguir riendo: He laughed away like a fool long after the others had stopped.

laugh down **ridiculizar:** Bruce laughed down his sister's attempts to appear important.

laugh off **quitar importancia a un asunto (riendo):** She apologized for ignoring him but he laughed it off and said it was nothing.

laugh on **seguir riendo:** Robert laughed on at the comedian's joke although it wasn't very funny.

laugh over **reírse de (un chiste):** They were laughing over the story an Australian told about a kangaroo.

lay about **dar golpes (a diestro y siniestro):** When the ruffians attacked the shopkeeper, he laid about them vigorously.

lay away **guardar (dinero):** My father says that I should lay some money away for a rainy day.

lay by **ahorrar:** Wise people lay by a little money each month if they are able.
apartar: The man laid the book by and went to switch on the television.

lay down **poner (en el suelo):** The woodman laid down the bundle of firewood and lit his pipe.
dejar (dinero en depósito): He had to lay down a lot of money as a deposit.
sacrificar (la vida): What a lot of people have laid down their lives for unworthy causes!
apostar (dinero): He laid down fifty pounds on the favourite in the three-thirty race.
establecer (normas): The headmaster has laid down new rules about work in the afternoon.
abandonar (una esperanza): They laid down all hope when they heard the bad news.
deponer (las armas): The defeated troops were called on to lay down their arms.

lay in **almacenar:** Our neighbours laid in a large supply of food for the winter.

lay into **dar golpes a:** He laid into his assailant and left him begging for mercy.

lay it on **exagerar:** He lays it on a bit too much in his efforts to please.

lay off **despedir (del trabajo):** The local car factory has just laid off a thousand workers.
dejar de hacer algo: He only laid off hitting her when the police arrived.
abstenerse de: The doctor told him he'd have to lay off drink for a while.

lay on **pegar (dar golpes):** The old lady laid several blows with her umbrella on her assailant.
instalar: The Wilsons are getting the electricity laid on soon.
dar una mano (de pintura): You'll have to lay on another coat of paint there.
colocar sobre: She laid newspapers on the floor over the damp patch.
imponer: There was a severe tax laid on the rebellious people.

lay out **trazar (diseñar):** The architect laid out the plans for the new town hall.
exponer (para la venta): The street vendor laid his wares out on the pavement.
amortajar: The corpse was laid out ready for burial.
dejar inconsciente: Tom Smith laid his opponent out with a blow.
exponer (ideas): He laid his arguments out for everyone to study.
marcar: They followed the lines which were already laid out.
invertir (dinero): He's now getting dividends on the money he laid out.

lay over **extender sobre:** She tenderly laid the blanket over the sleeping child.

lay up **guardar:** Some of the things were laid up for future use.

estar enfermo en cama: He was laid up with the "flu" for three weeks.
retirar del servicio (un buque): The ship was laid up while it underwent repairs.
atesorar: Christ told his disciples it was better to lay up treasures in heaven than on earth.
ahorrar: They laid up quite a bit of money to buy a new house.

lead along **guiar por (a lo largo de):** He led the horse along the fence and tied him to a post.

lead down **guiar (yendo hacia abajo):** The guide will lead the party of climbers down safely.

lead in **guiar (yendo hacia adentro):** The teacher led the children in when it began to rain.

lead into **guiar (yendo hacia adentro):** The suspect was led into the police station.

lead off **guiar (abandonando un lugar):** Mr Grimes led off and the boys unwillingly followed.
empezar: I will lead off by asking the students the first question.

lead on **seguir adelante:** Lead on, Mr Wright, and we'll follow you.
guiar (mostrando el camino): The guide led them on, never doubting for a moment where he was going.
ejercer influencia sobre: She was always leading him on and then was surprised when he made a pass.
hacer creer: They led him on to believe that she was in love with him.

lead out **guiar (yendo hacia afuera):** The teacher led the children out.

lead up **guiar (yendo hacia arriba):** They asked the climber to lead them up the mountain.

lead up to **preparar el camino para (un asunto):** He led up to the question of the loan by various hints about his financial problems.

leak out **infiltrarse:** When the news of the pending take-over leaked out, the shares went up.

leak out of **rezumar de:** The wine leaked out of the old casks.

lean back **recostarse:** The old countryman leaned back against the grassy bank and lit his pipe.

lean on **apoyarse sobre:** She leaned her head on the young man's shoulder.

lean out **asomarse:** The woman leaned out too far and fell to the ground.

lean out of **asomarse a:** It is dangerous to lean out of the window of a moving train.

lean over **inclinarse por encima de:** The two travellers leaned over the parapet of the bridge and gazed at the limpid water below.

leap over **saltar por encima de:** In the high jump you have to leap over a horizontal bar placed at a certain height.

leap up **dar un salto:** The cat leapt up on the table and began drinking the milk.

leave off **dejar de:** At what time do you leave off work?
parar: When the rain leaves off, we'll go out for a walk.
dejar de usar (ropa): People leave their overcoats off in good weather.

leave on **dejar (encendido):** Don´t leave the lights on when you go out of the office.

leave out **excluir:** Don't leave me out when you are making up your party list.

leave over **dejar para más tarde:** We'll leave this fish over for tomorrow.

lend out **prestar:** He said he would lend it out on the condition that it was returned undamaged.
alquilar (dejar en alquiler): He lent his bicycle out for a pound a day.

let by **dejar pasar:** The people stepped aside to let the cyclists by.

let down **dejar bajar:** They let the dog down into the rabbit burrow and waited with their guns ready.
dejar plantado: She promised to go to the dance with him but at the last minute she let him down and went with someone else.
soltarse (el pelo): When she lets her hair down she really enjoys herself.

let in **dejar entrar:** The dog is waiting outside the door; let it in.
ser timado: In spite of his experience, he got let in for five pounds.

let in on **revelar (un secreto):** They wouldn't let her in on the secret because she wasn't to be trusted.
compartir (un secreto): We'll let you in on this on the condition you don't breathe a word.

let into **dejar entrar en:** Before she let him into the house she made him clean his feet on the doormat.
incrustar en: The plaque was let into the wall of the house.
dar a conocer: If you promise not to tell anybody, I'll let you into the secret.

let off **soltar:** The boy let the balloons off and watched them float away.
disparar (hacer una descarga): They let their guns off as a signal that they had found the body.
excusar: We'll let you off this time but next time you'll have to buy the drinks.

hacer explotar: The bomb was let off with a huge explosion and a lot of smoke.
lanzar (fuegos artificiales): The mayor told the boys not to let off any more fireworks.
amonestar: The magistrate let him off with a caution on account of his youth.

let on **revelar (un secreto):** He didn't want to let on about his sister's marriage as it was a secret.

let out **dejar salir:** Let me out, please!
soltar: The boy opened the cage and let the canary out.
revelar (un secreto): She accidentally let out that she had run up a bill in the shop.
ensanchar (una prenda): As her dress was too tight, she let it out.
alquilar (dejar en alquiler): She lets rooms out to students.
pegar (a diestro y siniestro): The cornered man let out in a fury at his tormentors.
lanzar (un grito): She let out a cry of fright and alarm when she saw the mouse.

let out at **atacar a (verbalmente):** She let out at him over a very trivial matter.

let out of **dejar salir de (un lugar a alguien retenido):** Nobody was let out of the room until the examination was over.

let up **disminuir:** He's been able to walk about a bit since the pain in his legs let up.
dejar subir: The men said that they had an appointment with the doctor on the first floor, so the doorman let them up.

lick off **chuparse (los dedos al comer):** Bobby licked the sauce off his fingers after eating the chicken.

lick up **lamer totalmente:** The cat quickly licked up the spilt milk.

lie by **tumbarse al lado de:** She lay by the side of her sleeping husband and worried about a thousand little things.

lie down **echarse:** He lay down on the grass and watched the birds flying overhead.

lie in **quedarse en cama:** He always lies in on a Sunday morning.

lie over **quedar en suspenso:** The business had to lie over until there was more time to discuss it.
descansar sobre: The tree trunk lay over the stream where it had fallen.

lie to **permanecer parado (un barco):** The ship lay to on a sea as smooth as glass.

lie under **estar en poder de:** That country lay under a cruel tyranny for more than ten years.
estar bajo (una maldición): The land lay under a curse and produced nothing but weeds.

lie up **recuperarse (de una enfermedad):** The doctor told Tom he would have to lie up for some time after his attack of influenza.
permanecer inactivo (un buque): The ship will have to lie up in dock until it is repaired.

lift up **levantar:** The father lifted the boy up on his shoulders so that he could see the procession passing.

light into **arremeter contra:** The tramp was afraid the angry farmer would light into him.

light on **dar con (encontrar por casualidad):** When I was in the antique shop, I happened to light on an old ormolu clock.

light out **huir:** He lit out for distant parts and was not heard of again.

light up **encender:** The two farmers lit up their pipes and sat down on a grassy bank.
iluminarse (la cara de alegría): Her face lit up with joy when she heard her lover's voice.

line off **demarcar:** The farmer lined off the part of the field he intended to use for cabbage.

line up **alinearse:** The two teams lined up while the band played the national anthem.

link up **unir:** Those camps are linked up by telephone.

listen in **escuchar (la radio):** Everybody had the radio on and was listening in to hear the Prime Minister's words.

listen to **escuchar:** Listen to the song of the birds; isn't it a beautiful sound?

live down **vivir (honradamente para que el pasado se olvide):** It is very difficult to live down a scandal in one's past life.

live on **vivir a expensas de (sentido peyorativo):** As Tim Slater has not got a job he lives on his parents' generosity.
seguir viviendo: In spite of many illnesses he lived on to the ripe old age of ninety.
vivir (alimentarse) de: The inhabitants of some countries live almost entirely on a diet of rice.

live out **sobrevivir (a alguien):** "I'll live you out, strong as you are", she threatened, and she did.
vivir (lejos del trabajo): Most students live out nowadays, few of them live in.

live it up **darse la gran vida:** If I win that money, I'll live it up.

loaded down **cargado:** The woman was loaded down with a heavy shopping basket.

load up **cargar (un vehículo):** I saw two men loading the lorry up with bricks.

lock in **poner bajo llave:** They locked the cat in the house when they went to work in the fields.

lock out **cerrar la puerta (a alguien):** I thought that I was locked out but I saw the key above the door.
encontrarse en la calle (por estar la puerta cerrada): The lodger found himself locked out and his cases left beside the gate.

lock up **cerrar con llave:** The manager locked the bank up after everybody had left.
encarcelar: He was locked up because he was considered a public danger.

look about **mirar alrededor:** He turned his head and looked about him with surprise.
estar al tanto: "Look about it and don't stand there all day!", said the sergeant.

look about for **buscar:** I hear you're looking about for a job; I hope you'll be lucky.

look after **cuidar de:** Her sister looks after the children in the evenings.
cuidarse de: He told us not to worry, because he could look after himself.
seguir con la vista: The old man looked after every pretty girl that passed in the street.

look around **mirar alrededor:** She looked around to see if she'd forgotten anything.

look around for **buscar:** They are looking around for a flat as they intend getting married.

look at **mirar:** What are you looking at?
fijarse en: Look at the case of Mr Smith; this medicine worked wonders with him.
considerar: You must look at things from a different viewpoint.

look away **apartar la mirada:** The moment I looked away, the child ran out into the street.

look back **mirar hacia atrás:** The emigrants looked back nostalgically at the land they were leaving.
volverse atrás (en una decisión): Once he made his mind up he never looked back.

look back on **recordar:** He doesn't want to look back on their happy times together.
considerar (el pasado): Looking back on what's happened, I'd say we were wrong.

look down **mirar hacia abajo:** The aircraft passengers looked down at the lights of the city.

look down on **mirar con desprecio a:** You mustn't look down on any help, however small.

look for **buscar:** I'm looking for the pen I've lost.
esperar (tener esperanza): The results were better than had been looked for.
esperar (estar a la espera): The change we had been looking for came about.

look forward to **desear:** We are looking forward to hearing from you.

look in **hacer una corta visita al pasar:** As we were passing, we thought we'd look in and say hallo.
mirar dentro: He opened the door and looked in, but the room was empty.

look in on **visitar a:** They looked in on me the last time they were here.

look into **mirar dentro de:** She looked into the bag to see if it was empty.
investigar: The Post Office are looking into the matter of the missing letter.

look on **considerar:** All the pupils looked on their teacher as a friend.
mirar (como espectador): A crowd looked on impassively as the two men fought in the street.

look onto **dar (una ventana a un lugar):** The back windows of the house look onto the garden.

look out **mirar hacia afuera:** When there was a sudden noise in the street, the woman opened the door and looked out.
tener cuidado: Look out, there's a car coming!
elegir (después de examinar): She was looking out a new dress for the party.

look out for **buscar:** She told him to look out for her at the station.
estar atento: Look out for mistakes when you're reading the proofs.

look out on **dar (una ventana a un lugar):** Our house looks out on the sea.

look out onto **dar (una ventana a un lugar):** The top window of their house looks out onto the river Thames.

look out over **dar (una habitación a un lugar):** My hotel room looked out over the beach.

look over **examinar (con la vista):** She looked him over coolly from head to foot before replying.
mirar por encima de: The boy tried to look over the wall into the garden.
repasar: He looked over the report before sending if for publication.
dar (una ventana a un lugar): My window looks over the street.

look round **comparar:** It's a good idea to look round before deciding to buy a house.
volver la cabeza (para mirar): Everybody looked round when the pretty girl passed.

look through **rebuscar entre:** I had to look through various documents to find what I wanted.
mirar a través de: He looked through a hole in the fence.

look to **ocuparse de:** You must look to your part of the business and I'll look to mine.
recurrir a: When we are in trouble, we look to our friends for help.
tener cuidado de que: Look to it that the dog does not escape again.

look up **mirar hacia arriba:** They all looked up when the plane passed.
buscar (una palabra en el diccionario): If you don't understand the word, look it up in the dictionary.
mejorar (una situación): Things are looking up since I got the new job.
visitar: While you're in Birmingham, do look the Browns up, I'm sure they will be pleased to see you.

look up and down **mirar de arriba abajo:** When the man entered for the interview, the personnel officer looked him up and down.

look up to **respetar:** She looked up to her father but had little respect for her mother.

look upon **considerar:** The whole family looked upon their father as a tyrant.

lose out **salir perdiendo:** I think my brother has lost out on the deal after all.

lunch in **comer en casa:** On your way home, buy some slices of cooked meat. I'll have to lunch in today as I have a lot of work to do.

lunch out **comer fuera de casa:** I shan't be back home before three o'clock as I have to lunch out with my boss today.

M

make after **correr tras de:** When the hare was let loose, the dogs made after it.

make at **atacar:** The infuriated man made at his aggressor with a stick.

make away **escapar:** He struggled and made away despite the policeman's efforts to hold him.

make away with **escaparse con (algo robado):** The thief made away with a fat turkey.
deshacerse de: The dictator made away with his rivals.
malgastar: He made away not only with his own money but also with his wife's.
suicidarse: When the financial scandal broke, the banker made away with himself.

make for **ir decididamente hacia:** Where are you making for?
confirmar: This makes for what I've said.
ayudar: These excellent drawings make for an easier understanding of the text.
contribuir a: The speaker's words make for greater optimism.

make into **transformar en:** Heat makes water into steam.

make it up **hacer las paces:** They haven't made it up after their last row.

make of **sacar una conclusión de:** What do you make of the minister's latest statements?

make off **huir:** The burglar made off as the police were about to catch him.
marcharse deprisa: Without another word he turned on his heels and made off.

make off with **escapar con:** The shop assistant made off with the day's takings and disappeared.

make on **sacar provecho de:** The firm made on the takeover and subsequent new sales policy.

make out **descifrar:** I can't make out Joe's handwriting.
sacar en conclusión: The only thing I can make out from what he's said is that he's in trouble.
divisar: The castaways made out a ship in the distance.
entender: Can you make out what that woman is saying?
hacer (una lista): Make out a list of the things you want in the shop.
extender (un talón): Who shall I make the cheque out to?
fingir: The boy stayed in bed making out that he was ill.
arreglárselas (uno): He'll make out all right without our help.
redactar: I want you to make out a rough copy of your article before submitting it.

make out of **hacer (algo) de:** She made curtains out of the material she bought.
sacar en consecuencia de: What do you make out of this jumble of figures?

make over **ceder (traspasar):** Old Jones is going to make the business over to his son at his death.
hacer (una prenda de otra): The dress has been made over into a skirt and a blouse.

make up **redactar (una receta):** The doctor made up a prescription for my father.
preparar (una receta): He waited in the chemist's while the prescription was made up.
inventar (una historia): That story isn't true; you've made it up.
maquillarse: She spends a lot of time every day making up.
dar forma: She made up the dress in next to no time.
completar: The inclusion of Mr Jones makes up the total we wanted.
componer: He made up a poem about his experience.

hacer las paces: After the row they kissed and made up.
ajustar (una cuenta): You must make up what you owe.

make up for **compensar:** She tried to make up for her rudeness by behaving nicely.
recuperar: They made up for the lost time by working harder.

make up to **cortejar:** The men were making up to the pretty woman.
adular: They made up to him because of his wealth.
compensar: How can we make it up to you for the trouble you've taken?

mark down **anotar:** I want you to mark down what I'm going to say.
rebajar (el precio): The shopkeeper marked down the price from three pounds to two pounds fifty.

mark off **comprobar una lista:** They marked off all the items on the list.

mark out **limitar (con líneas):** The players marked out the field before beginning the football match.

mark out for **destinar para:** The youngest boy was marked out for the priesthood.

mash up **hacer puré (de patatas):** Mavis mashed up the potatoes for the children.

match up **recomponer (las piezas de algo roto):** It took me an hour to match up the pieces of the torn letter.

measure out **medir:** She measured the medicine out with a teaspoon.

measure up **tomar medidas (para hacer algo):** The tailor measured him up for a new suit.

mess up **ensuciar:** The baby spilled the paint and messed up the kitchen.
estropear (desorganizar): All our plans were messed up because of them.

mind out **tener cuidado:** You'll fall down the steps if you don't mind out.

miss out **omitir:** When they were drawing up the list they missed you out.

mix up **mezclar (confundiendo):** Don't mix up those English coins with these Spanish ones.
involucrar: She got mixed up in a scandal and got a bad name.
confundir: I mixed you up with someone I used to know.

mount up **acumularse:** Over the years their debts have mounted up alarmingly.

move about **ir de un sitio para otro:** While waiting he kept moving about because of the cold.

move along **seguir (no pararse):** The policeman told the onlookers to move along.

move away **alejarse:** She moved away a little from the mirror to get a good look at herself.
mudarse (de casa): The Smiths moved away from our neighbourhood last month.

move back **retroceder:** The boxer moved back before his opponent's attack.

move down **bajar (algo):** All the furniture was moved down to the waiting van.

move in **mudarse (instalarse en una casa nueva):** We went to call on our new neighbours when they moved in.

move into **meter en:** They move the flowerpots into the house in cold weather.
mudarse a (una casa nueva): When are you moving into your new house?

move off **alejarse:** The car moved off slowly and went round the corner.
quitar: She moved the vase off the table while she was dusting.

move on **circular (no pararse):** The policeman told the onlookers to move on.
pasar (a otro asunto): We've discussed serious topics enough; let's move on to lighter ones.

move out **mudarse (irse de una casa):** We're moving out very soon.

move out of **mudarse de (una casa):** The landlady told him to pack his bags and move out of the house.

move over **pasar por encima de:** The dark clouds moved slowly over the moon.
dejar sitio: Move over, darling. This is a double bed, you know!

move round **dar vueltas:** Don't keep moving round while I'm talking to you!

move to **mudarse a (un lugar):** Mr Black's firm is moving to Manchester.

move up **correrse (para dejar sitio):** Move up a little and let your grandmother sit down.
acercarse: He moved up close to the crowd to see what was going on.
avanzar (un puesto): He was moved up several places in the firm due to his good sales record.
subir: The level of the water in the ship's hold moved up inch by inch.

N

nail down **clavar (sujetar con clavos):** When the box was full the men nailed down the lid.

nail up **clavar (sujetar con clavos):** The notice was nailed up for all to see.
condenar clavando: The doors and windows in the deserted house were nailed up.

name after **poner (a alguien) el nombre de otra persona:** The boy is named after his grandfather.

narrow down to **reducir a:** The police narrowed down the number of suspects to two.

nose about **buscar (husmeando):** The dog nosed about looking for the rabbit.
curiosear: What are you nosing about here for?

nose into **entrometerse en:** I wish you'd stop nosing into other people's business.

nose out **descubrir (astutamente):** He nosed out some important facts in his investigation.

note down **anotar:** All the students noted down the professor's words.

O

observe on **hacer una observación:** Did your aunt observe on your unsual appearance?

offer up **ofrecer (plegarias):** We always offer our prayers up to the Lord.

open in **abrirse hacia adentro:** This door opens in, not out.

open into **conducir a:** The passage opened into a very big room.

open onto **dar a (una ventana):** The window in my room opened onto a beautiful view.

open out **abrirse hacia afuera:** Curiously, the door in that house opens out, not in.
desarrollarse: The stormy morning opened out into a fine day.
hacerse comunicativo: Once he started talking, he opened out and gave a lot of news.
desplegarse: The pink buds opened out into beautiful roses.

open up **abrirse (completamente):** From being a tight little bud, the flower opened up into a gorgeous bloom.
abrir (las puertas de un centro): The moment the store opened up, bargain hunters poured in.
abrir camino: It was the railroad system that really opened up the west of the United States.
sajar: The surgeon opened the patient up with a scalpel.
revelar: The recent spy scandal opened up the whole box of evil secrets.
abrirse paso (en negocios): The bank has decided to open up in South America, too.
hacerse accesible: After a few glasses of whisky he opened up and started talking.
abrir fuego: The guns opened up when the colonel gave the order.

hablar claramente: The man had been silent but now he suddenly opened up and told us what had happened.

order about **dar órdenes:** The new foreman is always ordering the workmen about.

order away **mandar (a alguien) que se vaya:** She ordered him away and told him not to come back.

order in **mandar (a alguien) que entre:** The mother ordered the children in to have their dinner.

order out **mandar (a alguien) que salga:** When one group was ordered out, another was ordered in.
echar (a alguien): He was ordered out of the residence after causing a fire.

own up **reconocer (la autoría de una cosa mal hecha):** When I asked Tommy whether he had eaten the sweets, he owned up at once.

P

pace about **ir de un lado para otro:** I couldn't sleep last night and paced about for almost three hours.

pace along **ir a lo largo de:** Last night I paced along the street, deep in thought.

pace off **medir con pasos:** The man paced off ten meters and then stopped to mark the position of the fence post.

pace out **medir por pasos:** One of the seconds paced out the distance between the duellists.

pack away **almacenar:** Some of my books have been packed away for years.

pack off **enviar rápidamente:** They packed the goods off to the customer.
marcharse: He packed off and was never seen again.

pack up **hacer (una maleta):** He packed up the suitcase and tied down the lid.
dejar el trabajo: I'm thinking of packing up and getting another job.
averiarse: Our car packed up soon after we'd bought it.

pass across **cruzar:** The boat passed slowly across the lake.

pass along **ir a lo largo de:** This road passes along the shore of a lake.
pasar al fondo: Pass along, please; more people want to get in!
pasar de mano en mano: The packet was passed along from hand to hand in the crowded store.

pass away **pasar y alejarse:** The thunderstorm passed away over the distant mountain.
disiparse: His fit of depression passed away when he heard the good news.
fallecer: My father passed away last spring.
pasar (el tiempo): He passed away the time dreaming like Don Quixote.

pass back **devolver:** The footballer passed the ball back to the goalkeeper.

pass by **pasar por:** I pass by the cinema on my way to work.
omitir: When the list was drawn up he was passed by.
dispensar: I'll pass you by this time but next time you'll have to contribute.

pass down **pasar (algo) de uno a otro que está más abajo:** The firemen passed the child down from the window of the burning house.

pass for **pasar por (ser tomado por):** The mother looks so young that she and her daughter could pass for sisters.

pass in **entrar:** Pass in and see the show!

pass off **pasar (una tempestad):** The storm passed off and the sun came out.
pasarse (una enfermedad): I hope your illness passes off soon.
tratar de pasar por (fingiendo): He tried to pass off as eighteen in order to get into the cinema.
pasar (una moneda falsa): The counterfeiter didn't succeed in passing off the spurious five-pound note.
tratar (algo) sin dar importancia: He passed the question off and went on to another.
transcurrir (el tiempo): The day passed off quietly.

pass on **pasar (una herencia) de una persona a otra:** The heirloom was passed on from father to son.
fallecer: Poor old Tom passed on last week.

pass out **desmayarse:** A lot of people passed out because of the heat.
marcharse: He passed out without saying a word and without closing the door.
graduarse (en los estudios): Their son passed out with honours at the military academy.
pasar (de moda): The craze for suede shoes passed out like all crazes.
morir: Mrs Bixby passed out last week.

pass over **pasar por encima de:** The enemy planes passed over the airfield dropping bombs.
perdonar: We'll pass over your rudeness this time but not again.
omitir: He was passed over inadvertently when the list was made.

pass over to **pasarse a:** The politician passed over to the opposition.

pass through **atravesar:** The bullet failed to pass through the thick glass.
pasar de un sitio a otro: Bruce passed through the doorway and entered the gloomy house.

pass to **pasar (algo) a (alguien):** Pass the sauce to this end of the table, please!

pass up **subir (algo a alguien que está más arriba):** The boy passed up the bicycle and the conductor put it on top of the bus.
dejar pasar (una oportunidad): I'm not going to pass up this opportunity of getting rich.

patch up **arreglar con parches:** She patched up a pair of old trousers for him to wear in the garden.
reconciliarse: They patched up their quarrel and became the best of friends.

pay away **seguir pagando:** He paid away for years but the debt seemed to get no smaller.
aflojar (una cuerda): They paid away enough rope to tie up the boat.

pay back **devolver (el dinero que se debe):** Len paid me back the money he owed me.
vengarse: "I'll pay you back for what you've done to me!" the gangster threatened.

pay down **pagar al contado:** I paid down three thousand pounds for the house.

pay for **pagar (por algo):** How much did you pay for the house?
pagar (por un error): He will pay for his foolishness.

pay in **ingresar (en un banco):** Each day's takings are paid in by the cashier.

pay off **liquidar (una cuenta):** I finally managed to pay the debt off.
pagar (a alguien y despedirle): The bicycle factory has paid off a lot of workers.
ser rentable: If you bought these stocks now they would pay off in a few years' time.
ajustar cuentas: The gangster chief paid off some old scores by having his enemies murdered.

pay out **aflojar (una cuerda):** The rescuers paid out rope to the stranded man.
pagar (a plazos): She's got to pay out twenty pounds a month for the washing machine.
desembolsar: I had to pay out five hundred pounds before they let me have the car.

pay over **transferir (dinero):** The money has to be paid over by the end of the month.

pay up **pagar (una deuda atrasada):** Due to a court order he had to pay up all he owed.

peg out **tender la ropa:** As it's sunny, I'll peg out the washing.

pick at **meterse con:** Why are you picking at him? He did nothing to you.
comer (melindrosamente): He picked at his food without any apparent appetite.

pick off **arrancar:** The boy picked the apples off the lowest branch of the tree.
matar (uno a uno): The sniper picked the enemy soldiers off one by one.

pick on **reñir:** When anything goes wrong she always picks on him.
meterse con: Those boys should stop picking on their fat companion.

pick out **escoger:** She picked out the most ridiculous hat in the shop.
arrancar: He picked the flower out by the roots.
distinguir: He picked her out among the crowd at the station.
marcar (resaltando): The rivers on the map were picked out in blue.

pick over **revolver (para escoger):** He picked over the objects on the stall before choosing one.

pick up **recoger (del suelo):** Pick up that rubber you just dropped!
rescatar: The last of the flood victims was picked up by an army helicopter.

reponerse (de salud): After a rest in the country his health picked up greatly.
recoger (a alguien en coche): When my daughter arrived last week, we took the car and picked her up at the station.
recobrar (velocidad): When we got on to the motorway we picked up speed.
descolgar (el telefono): She picked up the receiver and dialled a number.
coger (algo que está encima de una mesa): The man picked up the glass and drank all the contents.
aprender algo de un idioma: Did you pick up any Spanish while you were in Majorca?
adquirir (algo que se ha encontrado por casualidad): This figurine is something I picked up in the Portobello market.
captar por radio: Their call for help was picked up by a passing vessel.

piece up **componer (con trozos):** It was pieced up until it was complete.

pile up **amontonar:** The work has been piling up for the last few weeks.

pin down **fijar con alfileres:** We pinned the map down to prevent it blowing off the table in the draught.
hacer que alguien sea preciso: However hard we tried we couldn't pin him down to a definite statement of intention.

pin up **sujetar con alfileres:** My drawing was pinned up on the board as it was the best work.

plan out **planear (algo):** I planned the novel out before I began to write it.

plane down **planear (un avión):** I saw the aircraft planing down to land.
cepillar (la madera): A good carpenter planes any rough surfaces down.

play about **juguetear con:** He should stop playing about with that knife.

play away **jugar en campo contrario:** Our team are playing away next week.
perder en el juego: He played away a fortune and is now poor.

play down **quitar importancia:** The government played down the outburst of public discontent.
representar un papel (sin suficiente vehemencia): He rather played down the part of the wicked king.

play in **entrar al son de una banda:** The dignitaries were played in by the town band.

play off **burlarse de:** Bruce is always playing off poor old Mr Wilson, who is very thin.
enfrentar (a dos personas): She played the two rivals off against each other.
terminar (juegos, partidos, deportes): All the matches must be played off by the end of next week.

play on **seguir jugando:** The children played on until it was time for tea.
explotar (sacar provecho): He played on their feelings of pity to get money.
perturbar: The continuous noise of the machine plays on my nerves.

play out **salir al son de (una música):** The happy couple were played out of the church.
jugar hasta el final: They played the game out though the light was bad.
agotarse: He gave in when all his chances were played out.

play over **practicar una pieza musical:** She was playing over a piece I failed to recognize.

play up **hacer rabiar (a alguien):** The class played the teacher up.
poner interés en el juego: The coach told the team to play up.

play up to **adular:** Stop playing up to her!

pluck up **arrancar:** Yesterday I spent the whole morning plucking up the weeds in the path.

plug in **enchufar:** You'll have to plug the lamp in; otherwise we shan't be able to see anything.

plug up **tapar un agujero (con algo sólido):** The pipe must be plugged up, which is why the water cannot escape.

point away **señalar a lo lejos:** He pointed away to where a tree broke the line of the horizon.

point down **señalar hacia abajo:** The man pointed down at the river in the valley below.

point out **señalar destacando:** My brother opened a map and pointed out the best route to our destination.
hacer notar: May I point out that if you adopt that attitude we'll get nowhere?

point up **señalar hacia arriba:** He pointed up at the hill above them.

polish off **terminar rápidamente:** After the meal he polished off a whole plate of cherries.

polish up **dar brillo:** The maid was polishing the silver up in the kitchen.
revisar conocimientos: You'll have to polish up your French before the exam.

pop down **hacer una corta visita:** Do pop down and see us when you come to Madrid.

pop in **visitar inesperadamente:** I just popped in to see how you are keeping.
asomar inesperadamente: The little girl popped her head in at the door.
meter inesperadamente: When Pete opened his mouth to cry I popped a sweet in it.

pop off **morirse:** When the doctors had him cured, as they thought, he popped off, just like that.
irse: I must pop off to the shops, but I'll be back in a jiffy.

pop out **ausentarse (un momento):** Mr Martin has popped out for a moment, but he'll be back shortly.
escaparse (una palabra): The word popped out before she could stop herself.
asomar de repente: The bird popped its head out of the nest.

pop over **visitar (sin invitación):** Let's pop over and say hello to old Mrs Glynn.

pop up **asomar de repente:** When the teacher walked out of the apparently empty classroom, a boy's head popped up from behind a desk.

post up **colocar un cartel en un sitio visible:** He posted the notice up where all could see it.
tener informado: I'll keep you posted up with regard to developments.

pour down **llover a cántaros:** It poured down all evening and we couldn't go out.

pour in **entrar el agua (de la lluvia):** Rain has been pouring in through that hole all morning.
echar líquido (en un recipiente): When you make my tea, don't pour too much milk in.

pour off **vaciar vertiendo:** Before he ate the yoghurt, he poured off the liquid that had gathered on the top.

pour out **echar (un líquido):** The host poured out a generous measure of whisky for his guests.
salir en masa: The crowd poured out of the football ground, talking in loud voices.

pour over **verter sobre:** Johnny poured the sauce over his chips.

press back **hacer recular:** A barrier of police pressed the crowd back.

press down **apretar hacia abajo:** He pressed the switch down with his thumb.

press in **apretar hacia adentro:** When you press this button in, the mechanism begins working.

press on **ser constante:** However difficult, we must press on with our work.
avanzar (con determinación): They pressed on against the enemy forces with unflagging courage.

press out **sacar con fuerza:** The force of the emanating gases pressed out the sides of the container.
exprimir: She pressed out the last drop of juice from the orange.

puff away **echar bocanadas de humo:** My grandfather used to sit by the window puffing away at his pipe.

pull about **maltratar:** The little girl was pulling the doll about by one leg.

pull along **arrastrar tirando:** I bought Tim a toy dog that is pulled along the floor.

pull away **arrancar (violentamente):** When they pulled the bandages away, they could see that the wound was infected.
separarse (violentamente): Despite his efforts to retain her, she pulled away and ran for her bicycle.

pull back **hacer retroceder:** The garrison's offensive made the attackers pull back.
echar hacia atrás: Somebody pulled the boy back when he tried to get first in the queue.

pull down **derribar:** All the buildings in this street are being pulled down.
debilitar: A continuous series of illnesses pulled him down.
rebajar: After a lot of bargaining, he pulled down the price.
hacer bajar: The boy pulled the branch down and picked the apples off it.

pull in **tirar hacia adentro:** An arm shot out of a dark alley and pulled her in as she passed.
pararse junto a la acera (un vehículo): The car pulled in and a man got out.
entrar (un tren en la estación): The train was just pulling in when I arrived at the station.
refrenar: They were forced to pull in their advance.

pull off **arrancar:** They pulled the apples off the branch.
quitar (de un tirón): She pulled the cover off the bed.
llevar a cabo (algo difícil): In spite of difficulties he pulled the feat off.
llevarse (un premio): You say he got a prize! How did he pull it off?

pull on **ponerse (una prenda deprisa):** He pulled his coat on and left in a hurry.

pull out **sacar:** He put his hand in his pocket and pulled out a handkerchief.
extraer: The dentist pulled out the wrong tooth.
separarse de la acera (un vehículo): The car pulled out and nearly ran into a cyclist.
echarse atrás (en un acuerdo): Just as the deal was about to go through, Mr Ervin pulled out.

pull out of **sacar de:** She pulled a long cigarette out of a packet.
arrancar de: The gardener pulled the weeds out of the wall.
salir de (un tren de la estación): The train pulled slowly out of the station.

pull over **ponerse (una prenda por la cabeza):** You put a pullover on by pulling it over your head.
parar (un coche a un lado de la calzada): The policeman ordered the driver to pull over.

pull round **recobrarse (de una enfermedad):** The little boy pulled round after the illness.
hacer volver en sí: Miss Benson has fainted; try to pull her round.

pull through **recobrarse (de una enfermedad):** Although he was very ill, he pulled through somehow.
curar: Mr Thomas was at death's door but Dr Brown's care pulled him through and he got well.
salir (de una situación apurada): It was a difficult situation but he pulled through.
sacar (de una situación apurada): My grandfather pulled the business through and set it up again.

pull up **arrancar:** The strong man pulled the tree up by the roots.
parar (un coche): The car pulled up and a well-dressed woman got out.
regañar: The teacher pulled him up for using rude words.
mejorar: He has pulled up and is now doing as well as the rest of the class.
izar: They pulled the injured man up the side of the cliff.
acercar (una silla): Pull a chair up to the fire; it's a cold night.
subirse (los calcetines): Pull your socks up!

pump into **inflar (con bomba):** Compressed air was pumped into the tyre.

pump out **extraer (con bomba):** They pumped the oil out of the stranded Japanese tanker.

push along **marcharse:** You should be pushing along now; it's eleven o'clock.
empujar a lo largo de: The boy pushed his bicycle along the roadside.
darse prisa: You'll have to push along if you want to get there by night.

push away **apartar (empujando):** The man pushed his plate away saying he had eaten enough.
dar un empujón: The rugby player pushed his opponent away as he made for the line.

push back **empujar hacia atrás:** She pushed him back when he tried to kiss her.

rechazar: The enemy attack was pushed back on the outskirts of the city.

push down **empujar hacia abajo:** He pushed the contents of the box down and shut it quickly.
demoler: A bulldozer pushed down the old wall.
bajarse (los calcetines): The little girl pushed her socks down.

push in **empujar hacia adentro:** The lid of the box was pushed in by the weight of the stones on top.

push into **empujar hacia adentro:** Now you must push the plug into the socket.

push off **apartar:** She pushed the heavy blanket off and jumped out of bed.
marcharse: Well, I'd better be pushing off; I hear someone calling me.

push on **seguir adelante:** After their encounter with the bear, the wanderers pushed on into the expanse of pine forest.
apresurarse: We´d better push on and try to get home before the storm breaks.

push out **empujar hacia afuera:** The door was pushed out by the force of the water behind it.
sacar (el pecho): He pushed his chest out saying he was the best man there.

push out of **sacar de (empujando):** We'll have to push the car out of the garage.

push over **volcar:** The strikers pushed a bus over at the crossroads.

push through **abrirse camino (empujando):** The film star had to push through the crowd.

push up **empujar hacia arriba:** The old man pushed his bicycle up the hill.

put across **colocar cruzado:** The carpenter put one slat across the other.
hacer entender (algo a alguien): I wish I could put across to you the necessity of action.

put at **calcular en:** This case looks very heavy; I'd put its weight at near a hundred kilos.

put away **apartar:** He put the proffered drink away saying he had had enough.
comer o beber: He put away three helpings of Irish stew.
meter en (un asilo): She was put away in the asylum.
guardar (algo que no se usa): You can put the Christmas decorations away until next year.
ahorrar: They are putting money away for the flat they want to buy.

put back **poner en su sitio:** Put that book back where you found it.
atrasar (un reloj): Your watch is fast; put it back twenty minutes.
retrasar: He put his return back by one week.

put by **ahorrar:** How much money has he put by?
eludir (una cuestión): We shall have to face the problem; it cannot be put by indefinitely.

put down **anotar:** Can you put down the list of the things we need?
sofocar: The revolt was put down with fire and sword.
pagar (al contado): I had to put down all the money before I got the land.
deponer (las armas): The soldiers put down their arms and surrendered.
depositar: We put down a deposit of five hundred pounds.
dejar (algo en una mesa): He put the glass down on the table and wiped his lips.
clasificar: I put her down as too conceited for the position we were advertising.

put down for **tomar (a alguien) por:** One would put him down for a lawyer by the way he speaks.

put down to **achacar a:** I'd put his outburst of bad humour down to tiredness.
cargar (a la cuenta de alguien): The hotel bills were put down to the firm's expense account.

put forward **proponer:** His name was put forward as a candidate.
adelantar: Have you put your clock forward?

put in **meter:** The boy put his hands in his pockets.
hacer escala (un buque): The ship put in at the Port of Barcelona.
presentar (una reclamación, una solicitud): He put in a claim for the money.
designar (para un cargo): He was put in as day-shift foreman.
interrumpir: "What about James?", she put in.
dedicar tiempo: They put in a long time looking for the lost watch.
contribuir con: Mr Lewis put in a hundred pounds.
incluir: Can you put me in in that list?

put into **meter en:** The farmer put the pigs into the sty.
traducir al: Can you put that letter into French?
insertar en: The carpenter put a piece of timber into the hole.
arribar a: The ship will put into Southampton tomorrow morning.

put it on **exagerar:** He's always putting it on a little saying he is ruined.

put off **aplazar:** The meeting was put off due to rain.
partir (de un lugar): We're putting off from here just as soon as we can.
dar largas: She put him off with a vague promise.
quitar las ganas de (comer): The grease stains on the table cloth put him off his food.
zarpar: The ship put off with billowing sails.
apagar: He put off all the lights before going to bed.

dejar (viajeros un autobús): We told the conductor to put us off at the bridge.
distraer (la atención): The noise of cars put him completely off his golf game.
desanimar: Nothing we said would put him off coming with us.

put on **ponerse (una prenda):** He put his coat on and left the house.
encender: Put on the lights; it's too dark to read.
poner (una obra en un teatro): They're putting on a play by Rattigan in the local theatre.
adelantar (un reloj): Before the plane touched down, the passengers put their watches on an hour.
asumir (una actitud): She's always putting on airs and graces.
apostar: He put ten pounds on the favourite and lost.
aprovecharse de: I hope you don't think I'm putting on you.
poner (cara de): Don't put on that look of aggrieved innocence.

put out **sacar:** It's wrong to put out one's tongue at people.
echar (hojas, flores): The trees and plants put out new leaves in spring.
apagar: We put out the light when we go to bed.
dislocarse: He fell and put his elbow out of joint.
zarpar: Several boats put out to rescue the drowning man.
publicar: There was a statement put out to that effect some time ago.
incomodar: I hope our visit hasn't put you out.
invertir (dinero): He puts money out at high interest.
enfadarse: He'll be very put out if you say that to him.
molestarse (por otros): She put herself out a lot to make everything comfortable for us.
extender (una mano): The traffic policeman put out his hand and the cars stopped.

put over **hacerse entender:** The speaker put his ideas over very clearly.
anunciar: They are putting the new product over very well.

put through **llevar a cabo (un proyecto):** He put the piece of business through successfully.
poner en contacto (por teléfono): Can you put me through to Mr Darcy, please?
poner (a prueba): They put the new car through a series of tests.
dar curso (a una instancia): His application was put through without difficulty.

put to **ocasionar (molestias):** Buying the house put them to all sorts of trouble.
presentar (una moción): The motion was put to a vote.
hacer ver: He put it to them that the situation wasn't as rosy as it seemed.
poner a alguien a hacer una tarea: Being too young to do a man's work, he was put to sweeping floors at first.
buscar una utilidad: My wife has put those old curtains to good use as cushion covers.

put up **poner arriba:** He put the cases up on the rack.
levantar: The man put the ladder up against the wall.
alojarse: Where did you put up when you were in that town?
poner (en venta): The farm was put up for sale.
ofrecerse (como candidato): I believe he is putting up for Parliament in the coming elections.
cerrar (una navaja): Put that knife up!
subir (los precios): They always put the prices up before Christmas.
erigir: The building was put up in record time.
hacer público: When the notice was put up there was great excitement in the town.
proponer (para una elección): Who are the Socialists putting up for the bye-election?
aportar (un capital): A group of businessmen are putting up the money for the new factory.
colocar en sitio visible: He was told to put the poster up where everyone could see it.

put up to **incitar:** Somebody put the boy up to stealing the apples.

put up with **soportar:** I don't know how she can put up with him.

R

race along **ir muy deprisa:** He raced along to the meeting place afraid of being late.

race around **correr de un lado para otro:** Her guests were nearly due and Mavis had to race around clearing up the mess before they arrived.

race down **bajar muy deprisa:** The postman raced down the stairs.

race off **salir corriendo:** He raced off without waiting for an answer.

race up **subir muy deprisa:** The hooligan raced up the street with the policeman in pursuit.

rain off **suspender un acontecimiento al aire libre por la lluvia:** The football match was rained off today. They say it will be played next Sunday.

rake in **recoger el dinero en una mesa de juego:** As soon as number 20 came up, I raked in my winnings.

rake out **ahondar escarbando:** He raked out a hollow in the soft mould.

rake up **hacer un montón (con un rastrillo):** The gardener raked the leaves up into a pile.
desenterrar escarbando: The government doesn't want that old scandal raked up.

range up **alinear en orden:** The troops were ranged up in battle order.

reach across **tratar de alcanzar (algo que está al otro lado):** He reached across the table and gave the child a slap.

reach after **tratar de alcanzar (yendo detrás):** He reached after the passing girl but she had already gone out the door.

reach back **datar:** His family tree reaches back to the Conquest.

reach down **alcanzar algo para bajarlo:** Can you reach down that blue dictionary from the shelf?

reach for **tratar de alcanzar (con la mano):** The boy reached for the cherries but they were too high.

reach out **extender:** The bird reached out its long neck and peeked at my hand.

read down **leer de arriba a abajo (una lista):** He read down the list of names very quickly.

read for **estudiar (una carrera):** What degree are you reading for?

read from **deducir:** I read menace from the tone of his voice.

read off **leer con fluidez:** The teacher read off the list of names in next to no time.

read on **continuar leyendo:** The schoolmistress told the boy to read on to the end of the page.

read out **leer en voz alta:** Father read the letter out to the assembled family.

read over **leer cuidadosamente:** I want you to read this over and tell me what you think.
leer (un escrito) totalmente: The director read the report over before lunch.

read through **leer de cabo a rabo:** The actors read through the play before beginning rehearsals.

read up **estudiar (unas notas) diligentemente:** He read up on the customs of the people before visiting the country.

rear up **levantarse (un animal) sobre las dos patas traseras:** The horse reared up and threw the rider down.

reason out **razonar (hasta llegar a una conclusión):** They reasoned the matter out quietly.
hacer razonar (disuadiendo): They reasoned her out of the idea of abandoning the children.

reckon on **contar con:** We reckoned on them to do the cleaning, but they didn't.

reckon up **totalizar:** The shopkeeper reckoned the bill up rapidly.

rent out **alquilar (como propietario):** I'll rent out my house on the coast while I'm abroad.

ride about **cabalgar de acá para allá:** The cowboy rode about looking for the injured steer.

ride along **cabalgar por (a lo largo de):** They rode along by the river talking about the weather.

ride away **alejarse (a caballo, en bicicleta):** The horseman rode away into the sunset.

ride down **pisotear (con un caballo):** The pitiless nobles rode down the peasants that got in their way.

ride for **dirigirse a (a caballo, en bicicleta):** He rode for the town as fast as he could.

ride into **entrar en (a caballo, en bicicleta):** He rode into the stable without getting off his horse.

ride off **alejarse (a caballo, en bicicleta):** He got on his bicycle and rode off.

ride on **montar (a caballo, en bicicleta):** The two children rode on the little pony.
moverse sobre (un punto): The cylinder rides on this pivot.

ride out **salir (a caballo, en bicicleta):** She rides out every Sunday on this ancient bicycle.

ride over **arrollar (con un caballo):** The charging cavalry rode over the wounded soldiers.

ride round **ir (a caballo, en bicicleta) de acá para allá:** The new master rode round the estate and saw all the farms.

ring back **llamar por teléfono más tarde:** The secretary told me to ring back later as Mr Harris was not in.

ring for **llamar (por teléfono):** They rang for her but she wasn't in.

ring off **colgar el teléfono:** I'm sorry, I must ring off now; I hear somebody at the door.

ring up **llamar por teléfono:** You'll never guess who rang me up the other day!

rinse out **enjuagar:** He rinsed the bottle out before pouring the wine in.

rise up **rebelarse:** They rose up against their cruel oppressors.

roll about **rodar:** The footballer rolled about on the ground in pain.

roll along **rodar por:** The egg rolled along the table and fell off.
pasar (el tiempo): The days are rolling along and I've done nothing.

roll around **revolcarse:** The boxer rolled around on the canvas clutching his stomach.

roll away **llevarse rodando:** The workmen rolled the barrels away.
alejarse (una nube): The clouds rolled away and the sun came out.

roll by **pasar rodando:** They sat in the field and watched the tractors roll by on the road.
pasar (el tiempo): The years rolled by and Johnny Jones didn't get any younger.

roll down **bajar rodando:** The ball rolled down the hill.
hacer bajar rodando: She put the light on and rolled the blind down.

roll in **entrar:** They rolled in blind drunk and filthy.

roll into **meter rodando:** The man rolled the wheel of the tractor into the garage.
entrar (borracho) en: They rolled into the house at two o'clock this morning.

roll off **caerse rodando:** He kept putting the pencil on the chair and it kept rolling off.

roll on **revolcarse sobre:** The dog rolled on the soft grass of the lawn.
seguir rodando: The rock tumbled down the hill and rolled on across the plain.
pasar (el tiempo): The weeks rolled on without any let-up in the rain.
moverse a un paso inexorable: The great tide of mud and debris rolled on unstoppable.

roll out **salir rodando:** The ball rolled out of the court and onto the road.
allanar (con un rodillo): She rolled the pastry out before making the pie.
hablar sin altibajos: He rolled out the words of the song in a deep voice.
sacar rodando: Tim rolled the wheel of the tractor out of the garage.

roll over **caerse rodando:** The marbles rolled over the edge of the chair and fell to the floor.

roll up **enrollar:** She rolled the blind up and opened the window.
hacer un paquete: The shopkeeper rolled the piece of cloth up in brown paper.
arremangarse: The men rolled their sleeves up and began to work.
llegar: He rolled up just as the meeting ended.

root out **arrancar de raíz:** The gardener rooted the weeds out.
encontrar (después de buscar): I'll try to root out something suitable for you to wear at the party.
erradicar: The strict measures adopted by the Church didn't manage to root the heresy out.

root up **arrancar de raíz:** Wild pigs had rooted up all the newly planted young trees.

round off **completar:** He rounded the performance off with a song.

round on **volverse contra:** The boss rounded on him for answering back.

round up **reunir:** The cowboys rounded up the straying cattle.

rub along **ir tirando (viviendo):** He is just able to rub along on the money he gets as a grant.

rub away **quitar frotando:** She rubbed away all the finger marks from the window.

rub down **alisar:** He rubbed the wall down with glasspaper before painting.
secarse el cuerpo (frotando): After the bath he rubbed himself down with a hard towel.
limpiar un caballo (frotando): The squire asked the groom to rub the horse down.

rub into **hacer penetrar frotando:** The man rubbed the medicine into his swollen joints.

rub off **quitar frotando:** He rubbed the mud splashes off his trousers.
borrar: Unfortunately most of the figures had been rubbed off.

rub out **borrar:** They boy rubbed the drawing out and started to do it again.

rub over **alisar:** The man rubbed the door over with sandpaper before painting it.

rub up **sacar brillo frotando:** All the silver needs rubbing up.
repasar (conocimientos): You'll have to rub your German up if you want the job.
hacer enfadar: Oh dear! I'm afraid you rubbed them up the wrong way.

rule off **delimitar con una raya:** He ruled off the margins before beginning to draw.

rule out **excluir (de una lista):** You can rule them out; they won't be able to come to the wedding.
tachar con una raya: He ruled out what he had written and started again.

run about **corretear:** Stop running about and sit still!

run across **atravesar corriendo:** He ran across the meadow to head off the escaping animal.
encontrarse con (por casualidad): Who do you think I ran across in town the other day?

run against **chocar contra (deliberadamente):** He ran the car against a lamp-post and then tried to get the insurance company to foot the bill.

run along **correr por (a lo largo de):** The boxer ran along the roadway jabbing the air.

run at **correr hacia (agresivamente):** The dog ran at the tramp snarling.

run away **salir corriendo:** The boy stuck out his tongue and ran away.
fugarse: They ran away to Scotland to get married.
desbocarse: The horse took fright and ran away when the train passed.
marcharse rápidamente: Don't run away yet; I want to talk to you.

run away with **escaparse con:** He ran away with the boss's money.

consumir (el dinero en gastos): Doctors' fees run away with most of his salary.
dejarse llevar (por una emoción): Don't let that bad temper run away with you!

run back **volver corriendo:** The dog ran back with the pheasant in its mouth.

run by **pasar corriendo por:** They ran by the gate without stopping.

run down **bajar corriendo:** He ran down the stairs and out into the street.
hablar mal de: It's not nice to run people down with gossip and insinuations.
agotarse (batería): The clock's slow; it must have run down.
atropellar: He had to go into hospital when he was run down by a car.
capturar (a un fugitivo): The police ran him down in the suburbs.
ir a menos: The coal industry is running down.
escurrir (gotas): The raindrops ran down the window pane.
descargarse (una batería): I'll have to get the battery charged; it is run down.
estar mal de salud: He looks very run down and much weaker than he was.
colisionar (dos barcos): The liner ran the trawler down in the fog.

run for **correr en busca de:** The dog ran for the ball which the boy threw.
durar: The film runs for two and a half hours.
estar en cartel (una obra): The play ran for two months.

run in **entrar corriendo:** He opened the door and ran in without looking back.
arrestar: The police ran him in for dealing in stolen cars.
hacer una corta visita: Can you run in and see how Mrs Brown is keeping?

run into **meterse en (problemas):** If you don't watch your words, you'll run into trouble.
entrar corriendo en: The rabbit ran into the undergrowth when it saw the weasel.
chocar contra: He ran into the gatepost when he was reversing the car.
encontrarse con (por casualidad): I ran into a friend in the bookshop today.
alcanzar (varias ediciones): The book ran into three editions the first year.
ascender a (una cantidad): His salary runs into many thousands every year.

run off **salir corriendo:** The boy made a rude gesture at the teacher and ran off.
imprimir: The copies of the manifesto were run off and distributed the same day.
recitar: He ran off the whole poem without stopping for breath.
tocar (una pieza al piano): Let's see if you can run off this piece.
descarrilar: The train ran off the rails but luckily didn't turn over.
acabarse (un líquido): All our hot water has been run off, so no more baths today!
duplicar: Please ask your secretary to run off another fifty of these contract sheets.

run on **continuar corriendo:** The long-distance runner ran on despite the heat.
funcionar con: They say he invented a car that runs on paraffin.
versar sobre: The conversation ran on the subject of nuclear power.
continuar (un párrafo en otra página): The printer ran the paragraph on to the next page.
hablar sin parar: She's the kind of person who'll run on for hours about her children.

run out **salir corriendo (de un lugar):** When the door was opened the cat ran out.
agotarse (las existencias): Their water ran out when they were in the desert.
manar: As he turned over, his wound reopened and dark blood began to run out.
salirse (un líquido): All the wine ran out of the old wine skins, the moment they were cut open.
expirar (un alquiler, una licencia): The lease of the house ran out last week.

run over **pasar (la vista por un escrito):** He ran his eye over the report.
repasar: I'll have to run over my notes before the exam.
atropellar: He was run over by a car.
repetir: Shall we run over that scene again?
ir a casa de alguien: Run over and ask Mr Brown if he could lend me a hammer.
derramarse: The coffee ran over the rim of the cup and spilled on the table.
correr por encima de: The wolves ran over the frozen surface of the lake.
rebosar: The flood waters rose and ran over the river banks.
tocar (el piano con facilidad): She ran over the piece without any difficulty.

run through **atravesar corriendo:** The rabbit ran through the wheat, followed by the dog.
atravesar (un cuerpo con algo punzante): The needle ran through her thumb.
gastar rápidamente (una fortuna): They ran through the legacy in two years.
pasar (la vista por un escrito): Can you run through this list to see if it's correct?
peinar: The old man ran his fingers through his long hair.

run to **ascender (una cuenta):** The bill ran to several thousand pounds.
no bastar: My salary won't run to a second car.
tender a: He's running to fat with this easy life he has.
correr hacia: She ran to him with outstretched arms.

run up **subir corriendo:** Hares can run better up hills than down hills.
levantar (una construcción rápidamente): They ran the building up in record time.
izar: They ran up the flag and played the national anthem.
acumular: She ran up a fair debt in the shop without realizing it.
acercarse corriendo: He ran up to us and told us the news.
coser a máquina: She ran the dress up in a few hours.
trepar rápidamente: The vine ran up the wall in a matter of weeks.

rush about **ir deprisa de acá para allá:** He's always rushing about but never getting anywhere.

rush along **pasar a toda prisa por (a lo largo de):** She rushed along to the shop to catch it before closing time.

rush at **lanzarse sobre:** The dog rushed at the postman snarling.

rush away **irse con prisa:** She rushed away without saying goodbye.

rush back **volver rápidamente:** He rushes home from the office to have lunch and then has to rush back.

rush down **bajar rápidamente:** The boys rushed down the stairs and out to the street.

rush for **ir rápidamente a buscar:** When the dance was called, the boys rushed for the girls.

rush in **entrar a toda prisa:** Peter Jackson rushed in to say that the police were outside.

rush into **entrar apresuradamente en (mencionando el lugar):** The fireman rushed into the room and rescued the baby from the flames.

rush off **marcharse corriendo:** The children rushed off as soon as they saw the dog coming.

imprimir (a toda prisa): I think we'll have to rush off another fifty copies of the report.

rush on **seguir apresuradamente:** He rushed on to see if he could reach the town by nightfall.

rush out **salir rápidamente:** When the fire started, people jumped up and rushed out of the theatre in panic.

rush round **hacer una visita apresurada:** He rushed round to see his friends before returning to the city.

rush through **atravesar rápidamente:** They rushed through the forest with their hearts in their mouths.
despachar rápidamente: We've got to rush through these letters if we want to go home early.
lanzarse a través de: He rushed through the ring of his attackers and made good his escape.

rush up **subir rápidamente:** He rushed up the stairs when he heard the call for help.

S

sail across **cruzar navegando:** The liner sailed across the Atlantic in four days.

sail away **alejarse navegando:** The relatives stood waving as the little fishing fleet sailed away.

sail in **entrar navegando:** I'd like to see the fishing ships sail in, late this evening.

sail into **entrar navegando (mencionando adónde):** The yacht sailed into the harbour.

sail out **salir navegando:** The trawler sailed out of Lisbon for the fishing banks.

salt down **salar (conservar en sal):** They salted down most of the meat and fish for later use.

save up **ahorrar:** They are saving up to buy a house.

saw down **talar un árbol con una sierra:** They had to saw down the old tree in front of the house because it wasn't safe.

saw off **aserrar (separando):** If you don't want the table to wobble, you must saw an equal amount off each leg.

saw through **aserrar de un lado a otro.** The tree fell before they had completely sawn it through.

saw up **aserrar en trozos:** Mr White is sawing branches up for firewood.

scrape along **ir tirando (viviendo):** In spite of the husband's small salary, they manage to scrape along.

scrape off **quitar raspando:** They painter scraped the old paint off the door before repainting it.

scrape out **fregar raspando:** She scraped out the last of the soufflé and washed the dish.

scrape through **aprobar (un examen) por muy poco:** She didn't study much, but she scraped through the exam.

scrape up **reunir dinero con dificultad:** I think we can scrape up enough to buy the house.

scratch off **quitar raspando:** The cat had scratched the varnish off the table leg with its claws.

scratch out **borrar raspando:** He scratched out the first two lines of the letter and began again.

scratch up **rayar:** I didn't buy the table because the surface was completely scratched up.

scream for **gritar desesperadamente:** The trapped girl screamed for help.

scream out **gritar:** The injured man screamed out in agony when they tried to put him on a stretcher.

screw down **sujetar con tornillos:** He screwed the lid down on the box.

screw up **atornillar:** The carpenter screwed the bracket up against the shelf.
arrugar (un papel): She screwed the letter up into a ball and threw it away.
armarse de valor: My brother eventually screwed up courage and went to the dentist.

scrub out **limpiar restregando:** She was scrubbing the pots out with a lot of noise.

search for **buscar:** He searched for the will in the drawer.
registrar (para encontrar): They searched the woods for the lost children.

search out **descubrir (después de buscar):** He said he would search it out however difficult it was.

search through **buscar entre:** He searched through the documents until he found what he wanted.

see about **ocuparse de:** Will you see about the preparations for the party, please?

see into **considerar (un asunto):** The manager has promised to see into the matter for us.

see off **despedir (a alguien que se va):** Are you going to see me off at the station?

see out **acompañar hasta la salida:** Mr Hill was all smiles as he saw the rich client out.
resistir hasta el final: Though the match was bad we decided to see it out.
llevar a cabo: Now that I've started it, I'll see it out as soon as possible.

see over **ver por encima de:** Can you see over the top of that wall?
visitar (haciendo un recorrido): A bus-load of visitors came to see over the factory.

see through **ver a través de:** The hunters saw the deer through the leaves.
llegar a comprender: They never managed to see through the scheme I proposed.
llevar a cabo: They promised to see the project through to the end.
conocer (las intenciones de alguien): We saw through his game of pretended innocence.

see to **ocuparse de:** He saw to the visitors' comfort while she prepared lunch.

seek after **buscar:** At one time he was the most sought-after actor in Hollywood.

sell for **vender por (una cantidad):** How much did you sell your car for?

sell off **liquidar:** The fishmonger tried to sell off what was left from the day before.

sell out **vender (participación de negocio):** I hear T.C.D. has sold out to B.C.A.
agotarse (algo que se vende): When we arrived at the theatre, the tickets were all sold out.
traicionar: The bank robber sold his accomplices out in return for a free pardon.

sell up **vender (todo lo que uno posee):** He sold up and emigrated to the United States.
embargar: The bankrupt man was sold up by his creditors.

send along **despachar (mercancías):** They told her that they would send the goods along that day.

send away **encargar (traer algo de fuera):** I'm sending away for that book as I can't find it here.
despedir (a un empleado): When we realized how useless our gardener was, we sent him away and looked for somebody else.

send back **devolver:** The publisher sent his manuscript back and suggested some changes.

send down **enviar abajo:** Mrs Bellamy sent the plates down to the kitchen.

send down for **enviar a buscar (algo abajo):** Mr Bellamy sent down to the kitchen for more plates.

send down from **expulsar (a un estudiante):** He was sent down from Oxford for stealing a car.

send for **enviar (a alguien) a por:** The teacher sent a boy for some pencils.
mandar a buscar (a alguien): She is very ill; we'd better send someone for a doctor.

send in **enviar adentro:** The teacher sent the boys in when the bell rang.
echar (una instancia): August 20th is the last day for sending the application in.

send off **despachar:** They are very quick; they send the goods off as soon as they get the order.
despedir (para un viaje): They were sent off at the station with much merriment.
descalificar (a un jugador): The footballer was sent off for kicking an opponent.
mandar (a alguien) marcharse: She sent him off and told him to stop bothering her.

send on **remitir (correspondencia):** My former landlord sends on all the letters that come to my previous address.

send out **repartir:** They sent out wedding invitations to all their friends.
arrojar: The train sent out great blasts of smoke.
emitir: The stranded ship sent out distress signals every ten minutes.
echar (hojas): This tree will send out new leaves next spring.

send over **enviar:** Mrs Brown has kindly sent her little girl over with some roses from her garden.

send round **hacer circular:** The letter was sent round the office for all to read.
enviar (a alguien a buscar algo): I'll send my son round to fetch the books this evening.

send under **hundir:** A torpedo hit the ship and she was sent under.
quebrar (una empresa): The firm was sent under and never raised its head again.

send up **echar (hacia arriba):** The fire sent up sparks and smoke into the air.
lanzar (hacia arriba): They've just sent up a new rocket.
echar (brotes): The plant sent up three new shoots.
mandar subir: He phoned the hotel desk and asked them to send up a bottle of champagne.
mandar para aprobación: That will have to be sent up to the boss to get his OK.

serve out **servir (alimentos):** She served the soup out with great care.

serve up **servir (una comida por su orden):** Will you begin serving up the dinner, please?

set about **emprender:** He reflected carefully how he could best set about the task.

atacar: The villains set about the unwary traveller with sticks and stones.
ponerse (a hacer algo): The housewife set about the housework immediately the children had left for school.

set aside **ahorrar:** Everyone should set aside a little money for a rainy day.
no considerar: I suggest you set aside all other opinions and concentrate on what I have told you.

set at **azuzar:** The angry farmer set his dog at the marauding boys.

set back **retrasar:** The bad weather set back the plans for the regatta.
costar: The bill for the outing set me back a hundred pounds.
atrasar: Before the plane landed, the passengers set their watches back two hours.

set by **ahorrar:** My father set some money by each month for when he should retire.

set down **colocar:** The hostess set the laden tray down carefully on the small table.
poner por escrito: Everything the suspect said was set down in writing.
dejar (pasajeros un vehículo): The bus set us down at the stop near the bridge.
establecer (normas): The rules were set down just as I had written them.

set down to **atribuir a:** His parents set down his failure at school to the harmful influence of his companions.

set in **caer (la noche):** Night was setting in as we took the road leading to the coast.
afianzarse: Reaction against the dictador set in after the massacre of the strikers.
incrustar: She was given a beautiful ring with diamonds set in gold.
comenzar (una estación): Winter set in early that year with frost and snow long before Christmas.

set off **emprender (un viaje):** They set off for London at six in the morning.
iniciar: The political assassination set off a chain reaction.
resaltar: The glaring red of her lips set off the pallor of her face.
hacer reír: His witty remarks set us off into paroxysms.
hacer explotar: When the fireworks were set off, they lit up the night sky.
impulsar (a hacer algo): My remarks about travel set him off on a long rambling account of his holidays.

set on **atacar:** The tramp was set on by a heavily built man with a stick.
azuzar: The farmer set his dog on his neighbour's sheep.
estar decidido a: He was set on becoming the richest man in the town.

set out **emprender (un largo viaje):** We'll be setting out at eight in the morning.
exhibir (una mercancía): The shop assistant set the goods out in the shopwindow.
exponer (para dar a conocer): The rules and regulations were set out clearly for all to read.
adornar: She was all set out with lace and pretty ribbons.
proponerse hacer algo: He set out to become famous.

set out for **partir de viaje para:** The following morning they packed and set out for their final destination.

set to **ponerse a (hacer algo).** Jack and Jill set to quarrelling as soon as they met.
ponerse a comer (con ansia): We were so hungry that we set to as soon as the chicken was brought in.

set up **erigir:** They set up a cross in the place where the man had been killed.
causar: The bad weather set up some dangerous driving conditions.

instaurar (un gobierno): A new government was set up as quickly as possible.
establecerse (fundar un negocio): I hear that you're thinking of setting yourself up in business.
elevar (una protesta): The townspeople immediately set up a protest about the new motorway.
armar jaleo: All at once they set up such an outcry as I had never heard before.
equipar: My friend Peter set me up with all kinds of books ready for university.
crear una organización: A special committee was set up to supervise the expenses.

set upon **acometer:** The ruffians set upon the newcomer and beat him senseless.

settle down **acomodarse:** He settled down on the sofa with a book and a glass of lemonade.
establecerse: I hear Jones has settled down into a nice business in the City.
asentarse: The contents of the packet will settle down after some time.

settle down to **prepararse (para descansar):** After smoking a cigarette, he settled down to sleep.
disponerse (a hacer algo): When the children left for school, she settled down to write her diary.

settle in **instalarse (en un domicilio):** When we moved here it took us quite a time to settle in.

settle on **fijar (una fecha):** Have Vincent and Christine settled on a date for their wedding?
posarse (un ave): The eagle settled on the branch.

settle up **saldar (una cuenta):** The bill comes to fifty pounds for the three of us, so let's settle up now.

sew on **coser (un botón):** She sewed this button on for me.

sew up **coser (un rasgón):** There's a tear in this sleeve; can you sew it up?

shake down **hacer caer (algo) agitando:** The ball lodged in the tree, but the boy shook it down.
dormir en una cama improvisada: There's no bed; I'm afraid you'll have to shake down on the floor.

shake off **quitar sacudiendo:** There was a burr sticking to his hat, but he shook it off.
librarse de: The fugitive soon shook off his pursuers.

shake out **sacudir (para dar forma):** The sheets had been folded away for weeks, so she shook them out before making the bed.
sacudir (para quitar el polvo): There was dust in the bag, but she shook it out.

shake up **agitar:** The doctor told the patient to shake the medicine up before using it.
lanzar (de un lado a otro): The accident shook us up badly.

shave off **afeitarse:** I hear that Paul's shaved off his beard.

shoot across **atravesar a gran velocidad:** The hare shot across the meadow, followed by the dog.

shoot along **ir a gran velocidad por:** The cars shot along the racing track at great speed.

shoot at **disparar a:** People should not shoot at birds with air guns.

shoot away **salir disparado:** The dog shot away when the man unleashed it.
seguir disparando: The soldiers shot away despite the cease-fire order.

shoot back **devolver un disparo:** The robber shot at the policeman and the policeman shot back.
volver a toda velocidad: The dog shot back when it heard its master's whistle.

shoot by **pasar a toda velocidad por:** A group of boys shot by on their motorbikes, shouting and laughing.

shoot down **derribar de un disparo:** According to a military spokesman, twenty of the enemy's planes were shot down.

shoot in **entrar a toda velocidad:** When the door was opened, a frightened cat shot in.

shoot into **entrar a toda velocidad en:** The mouse shot into the hole with the cat after it.
chocar violentamente contra: The car got out of control and shot into the side of a truck.

shoot off **salir a toda velocidad:** The runners shot off as soon as they heard the starter's pistol.
disparar (un arma): When the raiders came into town, they shot their guns off.

shoot on **seguir disparando:** Shoot on until all your ammunition is finished!

shoot out **salir a toda velocidad:** As soon as I opened the cage, the bird shot out.
sacar violentamente: The boxer shot out his fist and hit his opponent on the jaw.

shoot out of **salir a toda velocidad de:** The bird shot out of the cage when the door was opened.

shoot up **salir disparado hacia arriba:** When I opened the box, the spring shot up and hit me in the face.
subir a toda velocidad: The monkey shot up a tree in terror.
crecer rápidamente: The wheat is shooting up, thanks to the rain.
disparar a diestro y siniestro: The gunmen shot up the town to terrify the citizens.
crecer: How your son has shot up in these two years! He's taller than I am now.

shout at **gritar a:** He's always shouting at his sister.

shout down **hacer callar a gritos:** The angry crowd shouted the speaker down.

shout out **gritar:** My classroom is very big. When I call the students' names they have to shout out to show they are present.

shout to **llamar a gritos:** I shouted to her, but she didn't hear me.

show in **hacer pasar (a alguien a una habitación):** When he called, he was shown in by a pretty, dark-eyed servant girl.

show into **hacer pasar (a alguien a una habitación):** Show Mr Roberts into the sitting-room and ask him to wait a few minutes.

show off **mostrar (atrayendo la atención):** The farmer liked showing off the horse he had bought.
alardear: You can't believe half what he says; he's always showing off.

show up **aparecer, acudir:** The last of the guests did not show up until midnight.
distinguirse: I'm afraid those colours don't show up well in this light.
poner en evidencia: Her foreign accent showed her up.
conducir (a alguien a las habitaciones de arriba): He asked his secretary to show the visitors up.

shut away **cerrar con llave:** She shut the jewel case away saying she wouldn't need it for a long time.

shut down **cerrar (con tapa):** The workers shut down the manhole cover and went for lunch.
cerrar (un negocio): I hear Smiths have shut down because of financial problems.
clausurar: That nuclear plant is to be shut down by the end of the end.

shut in **encerrar:** The shepherd shut the sheep in for the night.
rodear: The invading army shut them in on every side.

shut off **aislarse:** You shouldn't shut yourself off from all your friends and relatives.
cortar (una carretera): The road was shut off by a landslide.
cerrar (el agua, el gas): Don't forget to shut off the water and gas before you leave on holiday.

shut out **no dejar entrar:** They shut the dog out every night.

shut up **callarse:** Shut up; I'm not interested in your silly gossip!
clausurar (un negocio): The people who had the bakery shut up and moved because business was bad.
cerrar (una tienda por la noche): He shut up the shop and put the key in his pocket.
hacer callar: The teacher shut the talkative boys up with a severe look.
recluir: In the old days unmarried girls were often shut up in convents.

sing away **cantar alegremente:** Mavis was happy and was singing away in her room all morning.

sit back **acomodarse (en un sillón):** He sat back with a sigh of contentment and lit a cigar.

sit down **sentarse:** They told me to sit down and make myself at home.

sit for **presentarse (a un examen):** I can't remember when I last sat for an exam.
posar (como modelo): When you sit for an artist you must keep very still.

sit on **seguir sentado:** He sat on after the other visitors had left.
tomar parte en: He's an important man; he sits on several committees.

sit out **quedarse hasta el final:** We sat out the performance but we didn't enjoy ourselves.
quedarse sin bailar: She had been on her feet all the evening, so she wanted to sit this next dance out.

sit up **incorporarse (en la cama):** He sat up in bed yawning and putting off the moment of getting up.
trasnochar: Our neighbours used to sit up until the small hours talking and laughing.
incorporarse (después de una enfermedad): They were all pleased when the patient sat up and asked for chicken broth.
prestar atención: The news about the robbery made them all sit up and take notice.

sit up with **velar a:** The old lady sat up all night with the sick boy.

size up **juzgar:** I can't quite size him up; he's an enigma.

sleep away **pasar el tiempo durmiendo:** When he was young he used to sleep whole mornings away.

sleep in **quedarse dormido:** I'm sorry I was late for work today, but I'm afraid I slept in.

sleep it off **dormir (la mona un borracho):** When the drunken man was arrested, he slept it off in the police cell.

sleep off **liberarse de algo durmiendo:** He slept off the effects of the previous night's big dinner.

sleep on **continuar durmiendo:** The children slept on even after the postman came and went.

sleep on it **consultarlo con la almohada:** If you don't want to give your decision now, why not sleep on it and let me know in the morning?

slice up **cortar en rebanadas:** The housewife quickly sliced up the loaf and made sandwiches.

slip across **cruzar rápida y silenciosamente:** Silently he slipped across the room and opened the door.

slip along **pasar rápida y silenciosamente:** The mouse slipped along the bottom of the wall and disappeared into a hole.

slip away **marcharse rápida y silenciosamente:** The husband slipped away to the pub while his wife was telephoning her parents.

slip back **regresar rápida y silenciosamente:** The suspicious husband slipped back from the conference to spy on his wife.

slip down **bajar rápida y silenciosamente:** The gang of outlaws slipped down from their hideout in the hills to rob the bank.
deslizarse: The barefoot native slipped down the palm tree with a coconut clutched in one hand.
caerse (una prenda): She's become so thin that her skirt keeps slipping down.

slip in **entrar rápida y silenciosamente:** As the door was open a crack, the cat slipped in.
insertar: In his speech he managed to slip in a mention of his new book.

slip into **entrar rápida y silenciosamente en:** As the door was opened the cat slipped into the house.
meter rápidamente: The little boy quickly slipped a bar of chocolate into his pocket.
caer en (una falta): I see you're slipping into the habit of arriving late again.

slip off **quitarse (una prenda):** She slipped her dressing gown off and put on a green dress.
bajarse (de un caballo): The rider slipped off his horse before the tavern door and entered for a drink.
irse rápida y silenciosamente: The prisoner slipped off when the guard's back was turned.

slip on **ponerse rápidamente (una prenda):** He slipped a coat on and hurried out to catch the post.
resbalar sobre: The people in the cinema laughed when the fat man slipped on a banana peel.

slip out **salir rápida y silenciosamente:** The tenant slipped out with his suitcase when the landlady's door was closed.

escaparse (un secreto): She let it slip out that they were planning to get married.

slip up **subir rápida y silenciosamente:** It was late when Jack got home, so he took off his shoes and slipped upstairs to his room.
equivocarse: The secretary slipped up in sending the letter to the wrong firm.

slow down **aminorar la marcha:** Cars should slow down when entering a town.

smash up **destrozar:** The drunken rioters completely smashed the police station up.

smell out **olerse (sospechar):** The newspaperman was adept at smelling out social scandals.

smooth away **alisar:** This cream is supposed to smooth away wrinkles.
allanar (obstáculos): The legacy soon smoothed away their financial difficulties.

smooth down **calmar:** The special worker's comprehensive attitude smoothed down the man's ruffled temper.

snap up **comer rápidamente:** The dog snapped the food up as if it hadn't eaten for ages.
comprar (con ansia): The eager shoppers soon snapped up the cheap shoes.

snatch away **retirar apresuradamente:** Jane snatched her finger away from the hot water.

soak up **absorber:** The sponge soaked up the water on the floor.

sort out **clasificar:** I spent the whole morning sorting out the things that were stored up in the attic.
solucionar: My husband will soon sort that problem out for you!

speak for **defender hablando:** There are lots of minority groups with no one to speak for them.
hablar (en representación de): As the chairman had a cold, the vicechairman spoke for him.

speak out **hablar sin reparos:** The union leader spoke out against the exploitation of workers.
hablar claro y en alta voz: Speak out, man; the people at the back can't hear you!

speak up **levantar la voz (para hablar más alto):** The teacher told the timid girl to speak up, as he couldn't hear her.

speak up for **salir en defensa de:** When he was accused there was no one to speak up for him.

speed up **acelerar:** Once the driver had left the town, he was free to speed up.

spell out **deletrear:** He spelled his name out over the phone so that the girl should get it right.

spin out **alargar:** He has a habit of spinning stories out until people get bored.

split up **dividir:** Outside the town the robbers halted and split up the booty.

spread out **extenderse:** The advancing army spread out over the hill-side.

spread over **extender para tapar:** You should spread a clean piece of cloth over the glasses to keep the flies off.

spring at **abalanzarse sobre:** The weasel sprang at the frightened rabbit's throat.

spring away **alejarse de un salto:** The two dogs sprang away playfully and circled each other.

spring back **retroceder de un salto:** He sprang back in fright when he saw the face of the man he believed he had murdered.

spring down **bajar de un salto:** The young farmer sprang down from the cart and opened the gate.

spring in **entrar de un salto.** When I opened the door of the hut, a squirrel sprang in.

spring on **subirse de un salto:** The cowboy sprang nimbly on the horse's back.

spring out **salir de un salto:** When the cage door was opened, the kangaroo sprang out.
brotar (un manantial): A jet of clear water sprang out from the cleft in the rocks.

spring over **saltar por encima de:** The boys were trying to see if they could spring over the low wall.

spring up **levantarse de un salto:** The little man sprang up angrily when his wife threatened him with a roller.
brotar: It's amazing how quickly plants spring up in this part of the country.
surgir: Many heresies sprang up and died just as suddenly during the Middle Ages.
levantarse (la brisa): A cool breeze sprang up as night was falling.

stamp out **sofocar:** Any sign of rebellion was quickly stamped out.

stand about **rodear:** The invading army stood about the besieged town.
estar ocioso: Get working! You can't stand about all day doing nothing.
mantenerse cerca: He just stood about, wishing neither to go away nor to join the group.

stand along **estar alineado:** The railway workers stood along the tracks as the train passed.

stand away **mantenerse alejado:** He stood away from the picture trying to see it in the best light.

stand back **retroceder:** The crowd lining the route stood back to let the band pass.

stand by **estar al lado de:** The man was standing by the gate smoking.
apoyar (ayudar): I promise to stand by you, come what may.
estar alerta: The armed forces were told to stand by and await further orders.
no intervenir: The gang would vandalize the whole district, while the police stood by impassively.

stand down **renunciar (a un cargo):** When he stood down from his post as town planner, everyone was relieved.

stand for **tolerar:** Don't think for a minute that I'll stand for such behaviour.
significar: What do the initials USA stand for?

stand in for **sustituir a:** Mr Daly stood in for the leading actor while the latter was ill.

stand off **mantenerse distanciado:** He stood off and showed no signs of wishing to help.

stand on **estar de pie sobre:** The boy stood on the hill top and gazed on the valley below.
atenerse a: He was not one of those who stood on formality.

stand out **resaltar:** She is such a good student that she always stands out in class.
oponerse resueltamente: He was one of the few who stood out against any change in the company.
sobresalir: A rock stood out from the mountain face like a fleshy nose.

stand over **aplazar:** These matters will have to stand over till our next meeting.

vigilar: She stood over her children while they did their homework.
amenazar: The angry wife stood over her drunken husband with a roller.

stand up **ponerse de pie:** The people stood up and cheered when the aged senator entered.
erigirse: The huge gorilla stood up to his full height and thumped his chest.

stand up for **defender:** You will have to stand up for your point of view.

stand up to **hacer frente a:** The little boy valiantly stood up to the bully.
aguantar: He stood up to the test and came out with flying colours.

stand with **llevarse con (alguien):** How do you stand with your in-laws?

start after **partir en busca de:** The police started after the hooligans, but without much hope of capturing them.

start off **empezar.** Are you ready? Start off, then!
salir de viaje. They started off at eight the following morning.

start out **salir de viaje:** At what time are you starting out in the morning?

start up **poner en marcha:** He started up the car and kept the engine running.
dar un respingo: She started up in alarm when a floorboard creaked.

stay away **permanecer alejado:** The angry parent told the young man to stay away from his daughter.

stay back **quedarse atrás:** Stay back, please, the last of the runners hasn't come through yet!

stay by **permanecer al lado de:** He stayed by her through good and ill.

stay in **quedarse en casa:** The children stayed in to watch the telly.
tomar parte: The stakes are being raised to one hundred dollars in the next game; are you staying in?

stay off **no acercarse a:** Elderly cyclists are advised to stay off main roads, where they are in the greatest danger.

stay on **quedarse (en un sitio):** They stayed on to see what would happen.

stay out **estar fuera (de casa):** He usually stays out until the small hours of the morning.
no tomar parte: He decided to stay out to see if his luck would turn.

stay over **pernoctar:** It's late for you to go home, so why not stay over until tomorrow?

stay up **no acostarse:** They stayed up to watch the late boxing match on television.

step across **cruzar andando:** The old actor stepped sadly across the stage for the last time.

step away **alejarse andando:** She stepped away a few paces and then turned to look disdainfully at him.

step back **retroceder:** The boy stepped back in surprise when his father slapped him.
retirarse (para dejar pasar a alguien): I had to step back quickly onto the pavement to let a cyclist pass.

step by **pasar al lado de:** The burglar stepped silently by the sleeping dog with bated breath.

step down **bajar andando:** Dorothy stepped gracefully down the stairs swaying her shoulders.
retirarse (para favorecer a alguien): They asked him to step down in favour of the younger candidate.

step in **entrar andando:** The maid opened the door and an old man stepped in.
entrar por un momento (en un lugar): Shall we step in and have a cup of coffee?
intervenir: When things were looking worst, an American company stepped in with an offer of help.

step into **entrar andando en:** He stepped into the hall and wiped his feet on the mat.

step off **medir (con pasos):** The duellists stood by while the seconds stepped off the distance.
alejarse andando: He stepped off angrily muttering under his breath.

step out **salir andando:** The bouncer invited the man to step out and repeat what he had said.
apretar el paso: After strolling slowly for some time, they decided to step it out and see who would arrive first.

step over **pasar por encima de algo (sin pisarlo):** The passers-by stepped over the painting on the pavement.

step up **apresurarse:** The factory stepped up production the week before the strike.

step up to **acercarse andando a:** The brave man stepped up to the executioner and spat in his face.

stick at **persistir en:** Jimmy has not much imagination but he sticks at a thing until he finishes it.

stick away **mantenerse alejado:** He lived stuck away in the most god-forsaken part of the country.

stick back **volver a poner en su sitio:** After she had surreptitiously examined the envelope, the maid stuck the letter back in the rack.

stick by **ser fiel a:** I'll stick by what I said about Jones not being a person to trust.
quedarse al lado de: She stuck by her ailing parents and stayed with them to the last.

stick down **atascarse (sin poder subir):** The trap door seems to be stuck down and I can't open it.
pegar (adherir): You should stick the mat down at the edges to prevent people from tripping over.

stick in **prender (un alfiler):** You should stick this pin in to prevent the cloth from slipping.

stick into **clavarse (un alfiler):** While she was sewing, she accidentally stuck the needle into her finger.
meter dentro. The pickpocket stuck his hand into the lady's bag and took out a roll of notes.

stick out **sacar:** The boy stuck out his tongue when the teacher's back was turned.
asomar: Despite the warning, they stuck their heads out of the train window.
sobresalir: His nose sticks out like the prow of a battleship.

stick out for **insistir en:** In spite of the difficulties, he stuck out for the job and got it.

stick through **atravesar:** The swordsman stuck his rapier through his opponent's body.

stick to **aplicarse a:** He stuck to the job and finished it in record time.
permanecer leal a: We must stick to our ideals, or else we are lost.

stick up **sobresalir:** As she was running, she tripped on a root that was sticking up out of the ground.
colocar en sitio visible: He was told to stick the notice up in a place where it would be clearly visible.

levantar (la mano): When the teacher asked who had been smoking, Grimes stuck up a nicotine-stained hand.
sacar la cara (defender a alguien): When she went to complain, only her best friend stuck up for her.

stick with **ser fiel a:** Only the most loyal troops stuck with the losing army during the retreat.

stir up **armar (jaleo):** Some people delight in stirring up trouble.
agitar: With a stick, Jim stirred up the mud in the pond.

stop away **mantenerse alejado:** This meningitis scare has made many of the children stop away from school.

stop in **quedarse dentro (en casa):** He stopped in all day as he had a cold.

stop off **parar y bajarse (de un coche):** As soon as we see a restaurant, we'll stop off and have something to eat.

stop out **permanecer fuera (de casa):** He stopped out until the small hours of the morning.

stop over **hacer noche:** The Cranes stopped over at a little motel on their way to Las Vegas.

stop up **taponar:** He stopped up the bottle with a cork made of a piece of paper.
rellenar (un agujero): The stone mason stopped up the holes with mortar.
trasnochar: They stopped up as they were celebrating their son's arrival from America.

store up **almacenar:** Squirrels store up nuts to eat in winter.

stretch away **extenderse a lo lejos (un paisaje):** Bleak hills stretched away monotonously to the horizon.

stretch out **extenderse:** The branches of the tree stretched out over the road.

stretch over **extenderse cubriendo:** A dense fog stretched over the valley.

stretch up **levantar (el brazo para alcanzar algo):** The little boy stretched up in an effort to seize the apple.

strike back **devolver un golpe:** One's first reaction is to strike back when one is struck.

strike down **derribar de un golpe:** The blacksmith struck the insolent dandy down with a blow of his powerful hand.

strike in **interrumpir:** Peter Jones struck in with the remark that he was a good student.

strike off **quitar de un golpe:** He struck the doll's head off with one blow of his hand.
tachar: Dr Smith was struck off the register for unethical behaviour.

strike out **tachar:** He struck out what he had written and began the letter anew.
abrir (un negocio): He struck out on his own and made a lot of money.
abrir (camino): The group of hunters struck out a path through the jungle.
dar golpes (a diestro y siniestro): When one is in a tight corner, one tends to strike out wildly.

strike out at **golpear violentamente:** In his panic he struck out at the lifeguard who was trying to help him.

strike out for **dirigirse a:** They struck out for the hamlet which they were told lay behind the next hill.

strike up **dar un golpe hacia arriba:** The semi-conscious fighter struck up at the leering face above him.
tocar (una banda): The band struck up as the newly-weds entered.

hacer amistad: She struck up acquaintance with a businessman while on holiday.
comenzar (a cantar): They struck up a sentimental song about their native land.

struggle along **arreglárselas (uno) con dificultad:** Although nobody helped them, they managed to struggle along somehow.

stumble over **tropezar con:** As the boy was trying to slip out without being noticed, he stumbled over the doormat.

suck up **aspirar (absorbiendo):** This pump will suck up all the water in the hole.

sum up **resumir:** When you write an essay, it's a good idea to sum your ideas up in the last paragraph.

swallow up **engullir:** As he walked off, the fog swallowed him up.

swear off **renunciar a (mediante juramento):** Since his last illness he has sworn off drink and cigarettes.

sweep along **pasar rápidamente por:** The visiting potentate swept along the corridor and into the VIP room.

sweep away **barrer (eliminando):** Such feeble opposition was soon swept away by the triumphant revolutionaries.

sweep off **barrer (eliminando):** The wind swept the roof off the ill-made house.
quitar (el polvo): The dust was swept off the table.

sweep out **barrer (una habitación):** You'll have to sweep this room out; it hasn't been cleaned in ages.

sweep up **barrer (la suciedad):** One of them made the beds while the other swept up.

swell out **hinchar:** The wind swelled out the sails of the little boat.

swell up **hincharse:** When he sprained his wrist, it swelled up and he had to go to the doctor.

switch off **apagar:** Don't forget to switch off the telly and the light before you go to bed!

switch on **encender:** When one goes into a dark room, the first thing one does is to switch on the light.

switch over **cambiarse (de sitio):** Do you mind if we switch over? I'd like to sit near the window.

T

tail off **disminuir:** The sound of the man's retreating footsteps tailed off into the night.

take about **llevar (de un lado para otro):** She always takes that silly friend of hers about with her.

take after **parecerse a (entre familiares):** Some people say Johnny takes after his father, but I think he takes after his mother.

take along **acompañar:** If you wish I'll take you along to Mr Green's office.

take away **llevarse:** He used to leave his ladder in our garden, but he took it away last week.
quitar: Have some aspirin; it will take your headache away.

take away from **quitar de:** When he took his hand away from his lips, it was blood stained.
restar: If you take what you spend away from what you earn, you'll have little left.

take back **devolver (algo):** I'll have to take these books back to the library soon.

volver a emplear (a alguien): The firm promised to take the employee back after he had done his national service.
retractarse: I take back what I said about you being incompetent.

take down **bajar (llevar abajo):** Take down those suitcases; the next stop is ours.
apuntar (tomar notas): The secretary took down what the boss dictated to her.
humillar: The teacher took the arrogant student down by making him clean up the mess he had made.
derribar: That bridge will have to be taken down as it is no longer fit for use.
desmontar: The heavy machinery had to be taken down when the factory moved.

take for **tomar (a alguien) por (otra persona):** Excuse me for having spoken to you, I took you for a neighbour of mine.
tomar (una cosa) a cambio de (otra): Will you take my bicycle for your lawn-mower?

take from **quitar a (alguien algo):** The mother took the toy from one child and gave it to the other.
tomar de: Take the strawberries from this basket; they're better!

take in **meter (llevar adentro):** Take the bicycle in with you; don't leave it outside!
engañar: The salesman took in the woman with his talk.
meter (una prenda): She had to have all her dresses taken in as she had lost a lot of weight.
ingerir: He stopped eating as he just couldn't take in any more food.
admitir (huéspedes): She said she had stopped taking in guests as she had come into a bit of money.
entender: When he started using big words, we couldn't take in all he said.
recibir (una publicación): What newspapers do you take in?

coger (trabajo para hacer en casa): His wife takes in sewing and earns a lot of money.
incluir: Does what you say take in the cost of packing and insuring the goods?

take into **meter dentro de:** He took a pile of books into the bed with him.
hacer pasar (a una habitación): They took him into a waiting-room filled with people.

take off **quitar (una prenda):** Take off that boy's overcoat; he can't do it himself.
quitarse (una prenda): She took off her skirt and folded it over a chair.
llevarse: They've taken him off to have lunch at the club.
imitar (parodiando): He's very good at taking off famous politicians.
despegar (un avión): At what time does the plane for London take off?
marcharse: Take yourself off and don't bother us any more!
hacer una rebaja (de precio): The salesman refused to take a penny off the price of the carpet.

take on **admitir (a un empleado):** They're taking on part-time workers at Smith's factory.
cargar: The ship was taking on bales of cotton and tobacco.
desafiar: Despite being much smaller, the boy took on the school bully.
hacerse popular: The fashion for the mini-skirt took on in a very short time.
tomar (una responsabilidad): I should not like to take it on myself to bring up someone else's children.
ponerse fuera de sí: I don't know why he took on so when we mentioned his daughter.
emprender (una tarea): Do you think you can take the job on without problems?
aceptar (trabajo): Don't you think you've taken on too much with this new responsibility?

take out **sacar (llevar fuera):** It's your turn to take the dog out for a walk.
obtener (una documentación): Has your brother taken out insurance on his car yet?
retirar (dinero del banco): I'm going to the bank to take out some money.

take out of **sacar de (un sitio):** All their furniture was taken out of the house and left in the street.
quitar (una mancha): Could you recommend something to take grease stains out of clothes?

take over **tomar posesión:** Will the new government be taking over immediately?
hacerse cargo de: The army has taken over power in that country.
heredar (un negocio): Young Jones took over from his father when the latter retired at the age of sixty.
asumir (una responsabilidad): Robert was told to take over while Peter was having breakfast.

take to **llevar a:** The little green man pointed a ray-gun at me and said: "Take me to your leader!"
darse a: I'm afraid Brian has taken to drinking too much.
sentirse atraído por: Mary took to Albert the moment she set eyes on him.
dedicarse a: He stays in all evenings now he's taken to studying marketing.
adaptarse a: He took to it after a little while and began to get used to it.

take up **subir (llevar arriba):** The porter took their cases up to their room.
levantar: The blacksmith took up the heavy anvil in his arms.
descolgar (el teléfono): She took up the receiver hurriedly and said, "hello."
seguir (una profesión): Why don't you take up management? There's a great future in it.

ocupar (un puesto): The new minister will be taking up his post after the summer recess.
llenar (el tiempo): Don't take up your time with trifles; get down to the main business.
hacerse cargo de: My solicitor took up the case and did not cease until he had cleared it up.
recoger (pasajeros un vehículo): The bus took up three more passengers at the bridge.
absorber: The sponge took up most of the spilled water.
reanudar (un relato): The teacher took up the history lesson where he finished the day before.
acortar (una prenda): The skirt is rather long; I'll have to have it taken up.
adoptar (una actitud): If you take up that posture, there's no way of making you see sense.
patrocinar: His case looked hopeless until it was taken up by a parliamentary pressure group.

take up with **asociarse con:** He took up with the wrong crowd and went from bad to worse.
hacerse amigos: Where do you think she took up with him?
estar ocupado con: He's very taken up with motor mechanics just now and has no time for anything else.
plantear (un asunto) a: Why don't you take your complaint up with the manager? He'll be pleased to help you.

talk about **hablar de:** I don't know what you two are talking about but you are making a lot of noise.

talk at **sermonear:** I don't like the way he talked at me as if I were a stooge.

talk away **hablar sin parar:** She was still talking away after the last of the guests had left.
pasar el tiempo hablando: Pamela and Arthur talked the evening away.

talk back **contestar de forma insolente:** Don't talk back when you're being reprimanded!

talk down **no dejar intervenir (en la conversación):** Every time the poor wife tried to open her mouth, the husband rudely talked her down.

talk down to **hablar con desdén a:** On his first day in the office, the head of the department talked down to him as if he were a nobody.

talk of **hablar de (elegir un tema):** Let's talk of something pleasant, like the holidays.

talk on **hablar sobre (un asunto), dar una charla:** Our next lecturer, Mr Brown, is going to talk on Renaissance Art.
seguir hablando: Mrs Farthingale talked on and on until everybody was dizzy.

talk out **convencer (a alguien para que cambie de parecer):** Harry's friends talked him out of the idea of deserting his wife and emigrating to Australia.

talk over **hablar sobre (un proyecto):** The husband and wife talked over the idea of sending their son to a boarding school.

talk round **hacer cambiar de parecer:** He wasn't very willing to come on the excursion, but we talked him round.
hablar de un tema con rodeos: The committee talked round the problem of the firm's insolvency without mentioning it openly.

talk to **hablar con:** I was talking to an old friend of yours in the street yesterday.

tear across **rasgar en dos mitades:** Roger tore the letter across and threw it into the wastepaper basket.

tear along **ir a toda velocidad:** The motorbike tore along the road at 70 miles an hour.

tear away **quitar rasgando:** When we tore away the wallpaper, we saw that the wall was damp.

tear down **quitar rasgando (de arriba a abajo):** The angry shopkeeper tore down the poster that the students had stuck on the wall of the shop.
derribar: I hear they're tearing down the old public library and putting up a new one in its place.

tear off **arrancar rasgando:** The excited children tore the wrapping off the present.
quitarse violentamente: The bald man tore off his wig and furiously scratched his head.
salir corriendo: The boy tore off as soon as the class was over.

tear out **arrancar:** The struggling women tore each other's hair out in handfuls.

tear up **rasgar:** After he had finished reading the letter, he tore it up into small strips.
arrancar: The excavator tore up the soft earth and left a black strip in its wake.

tell about **contar sobre:** Tell us about the girl you went out with last night.

tell of **contar (hechos):** Jimmy was telling us of the time he was chased by a wild bull.
informar (con relación a una falta o error): The secretary told of the clerk's carelessness.

tell off **regañar:** The mother told the boy off for getting his clothes dirty.

tell on **chivarse:** I'll tell on you when daddy comes home from work.

test out **probar (hacer pruebas):** When Tom got his new motorbike, he took it out into the country to test it out.

thin out **aclarar (un terreno):** The farmer was thinning out the turnip drills so that the plants would grow strong.

think about **pensar de (opinar):** What do you think about our entry into the Common Market?
pensar en (considerar): When he asked her if she would marry him, she said she would think about it.

think of **pensar de (opinar):** What do you think of the new tax rise the minister spoke about?
pensar en: I was thinking of Gertrude when suddenly the phone rang, and it was her.

think out **llegar a una conclusión (después de reflexionar):** When he had thought it all out, he decided the best thing was to go to the police.

think over **pensar sobre (considerar):** The traveller spent a long time thinking over the things he would need for the journey.

think up **inventar:** The schoolboys were always thinking up ways of tormenting the science teacher.

throw about **tirar cosas (en desorden):** The burglars threw everything about in their search for jewelry and valuables.
tirar (una pelota): The team were throwing the ball about waiting for the game to start.

throw across **tirar a través de:** The boys were throwing the ball across the room.

throw away **tirar (algo inservible):** Mr Brown always throws the paper away when he has read it.
malgastar: Don't throw your money away; you never know when you'll need it.
perder (una oportunidad): If you throw away this opportunity, you may never get another.

throw back **devolver lanzando:** They threw the ball to me and I threw it back.
tirar hacia atrás: The force of the explosion threw him back against the wall.
traer a la memoria: The sight of the girl suddenly threw him back in time to one misty morning in Aberdeen.

throw down **tirar al suelo:** The nobleman threw down his glove as a challenge to the other man.
derribar: The bulldozer threw down the remaining wall of the house.
destruir: Whole forests were thrown down by the force of the wind.

throw in **echar adentro:** When the ball was thrown in, the game began once more.

throw into **echar adentro de:** They threw the shrieking girl into the swimming-pool.
meterse de lleno en (una tarea): He threw himself into the task and finished it in record time.

throw off **arrojar:** The rocket went up into the air throwing off sparks of all colours.
quitarse rápidamente (una prenda): The two men threw off their coats and began to fight.
librarse de: The detective succeeded in throwing off his pursuers.
escribir (sin esfuerzo): He's one of those writers who can throw off a short story in a night.

throw on **ponerse rápidamente (una prenda):** He jumped out of bed, threw on some clothes and raced down the stairs.

throw out **arrojar afuera:** The man was thrown out of the public house for disorderly behaviour.
tirar (algo inservible): Mrs Smith threw the old chairs out when they were no longer useful.
emitir: The satellite threw out signals which were picked up in the tracking station.
tirar (indirectas): She's always throwing out hints about getting married.
rechazar: The committee threw out the suggestions.
sugerir (ideas): There were so many ideas thrown out that it was difficult to choose one.

throw over **tapar (cubrir con algo):** She threw an extra blanket over the sleeping child.
abandonar: When his girlfriend threw him over, he took to drink.

throw to **tirar algo (para que alguien lo recoja):** Now throw the ball to me.

throw up **lanzar hacia arriba:** The men threw their hats up and cheered when the horse won.
vomitar: The dog threw up what it had eaten.
dimitir (de repente): I heard Jones threw his job up and told the boss to get lost.
levantar (un edificio): They've thrown this building up in record time.
desperdiciar (una buena ocasión): Don't throw this opportunity up or you may never get another.

thrust away **rechazar:** Jack thrust the plate away saying he could eat no more.

tick away **hacer tic-tac:** The bomb was ticking away four minutes before it exploded.

tick off **señalar (con una marca):** The jailer ticked off the names as the prisoners passed through the gate.
regañar: The father ticked off his son for taking his car without permission.

tick over **funcionar lentamente (un motor):** The car was waiting outside the bank with the engine ticking over.

tidy away **recoger:** Tim, Jane, please tidy your toys away before you leave.

tidy up **arreglar (poner en orden):** It's about time you tidied up this room; it's a proper mess!

tie down **sujetar (al suelo):** The cowboys tied the calves down before they branded them.

limitar: He was tied down to a choice between two unpleasant alternatives.
confinar: We're rather tied down in the evenings and don't seem to be able to get out.

tie in with **concordar con:** What you've said ties in with what Jim told me yesterday.

tie up **atar:** The packet was tied up with pink ribbon.

tip off **avisar sobre:** The hotel manager tipped the police off as to the whereabouts of the criminal.

tip over **volcar:** The jug was tipped over and the contents spilled on the table.

tire out **fatigar:** Working long hours tires a person out.

toss away **tirar descuidadamente:** After lighting his cigarette, he tossed away the lighted match.

toss off **tragar (de un golpe):** The fat man tossed off the glass of whisky as if it were water.
hacer (rápidamente): He tossed off a sonnet in no time.

toss up **echar a cara o cruz:** The referee tossed up the coin to see which team would kick off.
tirar a lo alto: Goya painted a scene of a bull tossing dogs up into the air.
levantar (la cabeza): The horse tossed up its head and stamped its hoof in anger.

touch at **hacer escala (un barco):** The ship touched at Suez on its way to Gibraltar.

touch down **tomar tierra (un avión):** The plane touched down on schedule at nine o'clock.

touch off **dar origen a (un debate, una pelea):** A remark by the leader of the opposition touched off a heated debate.

touch up **retocar:** The artist touched up the portrait before he handed it over.

touch upon **tocar (un tema):** During his talk the Prime Minister touched upon a lot of different topics.

track down **seguir (una pista hasta el final):** The police tracked the criminal down in spite of difficulties.
hallar (el origen de): After painstaking work he tracked the idea down to its source.

try on **probarse (una prenda):** She tried the dress on before deciding to buy it.

try out **probar (algo antes de comprarlo):** The idea sounds good but it would have to be tried out before being put into use.

tuck in **remeter (la ropa de la cama):** The mother tucked the boy in and said good night.
remeterse (la ropa): He likes his shirt to hang loose, not tucked in.

tuck up **arropar en la cama:** The parents did not sit down to supper until they had tucked the children up in bed.

tumble down **desplomarse:** Jack and Jill tumbled down the hill with empty pails.

tune in **sintonizar:** I tuned in to Radio Luxemburg last night.

tune up **afinar (un instrumento):** The violinist spent some time tuning up before he began to play.

turn about **dar media vuelta:** When he saw the policeman, he turned about and walked down a side street.

turn away **volver la cara:** She turned away for fear he should see her laughing.

marcharse (dando media vuelta): The man made as if to enter the house but he turned away at the last moment.
negarse a recibir: The Browns are a good family; they never turn a beggar away from their door.

turn back **volverse:** He turned back as he was leaving and kissed the children good-bye.
rechazar: The invading army was turned back at this point.

turn down **poner boca abajo:** He said it was his habit to turn the glass down after he had emptied it.
doblar hacia abajo: It's not a nice habit to turn down the pages of the book you're reading.
bajar (el volumen): Turn the television down, please; I want to make a phone call.
rechazar: The candidate was very crestfallen when the company turned him down.
dar calabazas (a un novio): After his girlfriend turned him down, he joined the army.
bajarse (el cuello de una prenda): Turn down the collar of your shirt; it's sticking up.

turn in **acostarse:** It's time to turn in; we've got to be up early in the morning.
doblar hacia adentro: He's rather ugly as the corner of his upper lip is turned in.
entregar (a la justicia): Although he was their son, they turned him in when he committed murder.

turn into **convertirse en:** She was surprised when she kissed the frog and it did not turn into a prince.
girar (en un coche): The driver turned into a side street and stopped the car.

turn off **cerrar (llave, grifo):** Did you turn off the gas before we left?
desviarse: Where do we have to turn off to take the Bristol Road?
expulsar: Intruders will be turned off this estate.

turn on **abrir (llave, grifo):** Have you turned on the bath water?
enfadarse con: The boss turned on the boy who had lost the money.

turn out **apagar:** Turn out that light and go to sleep.
vaciar (bolsillos): The security guard made him turn out his pockets.
producir: This factory turns out thousands of cars each year.
expulsar: The boy was turned out of the school for unruly behaviour.
reunirse: More than a thousand people turned out to hear him.
resultar: The exam turned out easier than we thought.
salir de casa: I wish I didn't have to turn out in this cold weather.

turn over **poner boca abajo:** The building labourer turned the cement mixer over and tapped the bottom with a shovel.
volcar: Their car turned over when it was hit by the truck.
reflexionar: I've just been turning over your advice.
pasar (un cargo a alguien): As he had too much on hand he turned the job over to me.
volver (una página): The pages rustled as he turned them over.
manejar (dinero): They turn over a lot of money in their business.
dar la vuelta: The swing went so high that it completely turned over.
entregar: A group of citizens turned the criminal over to the police.
dar vueltas: Henry turned over restlessly in bed trying to sleep.

turn round **volverse:** They turned round and looked at the land they were leaving.

turn to **ponerse (a trabajar):** They turned to and soon finished the job.
recurrir a: Who can I turn to in this hour of need?

empezar a: After it had stopped snowing, it turned to freezing.
convertirse en: With a slight rise in temperature snow turns to ice.
cambiar (de profesión): If you don't like painting, why don't you turn to carpentry?

turn up **presentarse (llegar):** Just when we had given her up for lost, she turned up in a taxi.
suceder: Don't worry; something is sure to turn up when you least expect it.
encontrar (algo en documentos): After a lot of searching he finally turned up what he wanted.
subirse (el cuello de una prenda): He turned up the collar of his coat against the cold.
abrir más (radio, gas): Turn up the radio, please; I can't hear it.

turn upon **depender de:** It all turns upon our being able or not to deliver the goods.
volverse contra: Even a cat will turn upon someone who attacks it.

U

use up **agotar:** When they had used up all the matches, they had to go out and buy more.

V

vote down **derrotar en una votación:** The government voted down the opposition's motion of censure.

W

wade into **ponerse a (hacer algo con ahinco):** There was a lot to be done but they waded into it and soon finished.

wait about **perder el tiempo:** How much longer am I supposed to wait about here?

wait at **servir (a la mesa):** Mary works waiting at tables in a City restaurant.

wait for **esperar:** They have been waiting for the train since two o'clock.

wait on **asistir (ayudando en las faenas de la casa):** There were four servants waiting on the fat duchess.
visitar (por negocios): Mr Slade called to say that he will not be able to wait on you on Friday morning at 10 o'clock.

wait up **esperar (a alguien levantado):** When Alec came home, he found both parents waiting up for him.

wake up **despertarse:** Wake up! It's a lovely day!

walk about **andar de acá para allá:** He always walks about when he has a problem on his mind.
dar una vuelta: The minister walked about through the fair chatting to the people.

walk across **atravesar andando:** The hardy travellers walked across the frozen lake.

walk along **andar por (a lo largo de):** The two lovers walked along the river talking of their future.

walk away **alejarse andando:** She looked scornfully at me and then walked away without saying a word.

walk away from **alejarse andando de:** As the postman was walking away from the gate, the dog bit him.

walk away with **marcharse con (algo robado):** The burglars walked away with Mrs Bell's life savings.

walk down **bajar andando:** It is easier to walk down the stairs than to walk up.

walk in **entrar andando (tranquilamente):** Look who's just walked in!

walk into **entrar andando en (un lugar):** They didn't know when they entered the forest that they were walking into a trap.

walk off **marcharse inesperadamente:** He walked off without a word and they never saw him again.
apartarse andando: The child keeps walking off every time I stop to talk to anyone.

walk off with **marcharse con (algo robado):** The man seated next to Mrs Wilson walked off with her handbag.
ganar fácilmente: Every year he just walks off with the first prize.

walk on **continuar andando:** Let's walk on until we get tired and then we'll sit under a tree.

walk out **salir andando (con indignación):** He slammed the door and walked out promising never to return.
ir a la huelga: The workers downed tools and walked out when overtime was stopped.
salir a pasear (dos novios): Did you know that Simon and Kate were walking out together?

walk out on **abandonar a:** He walked out on his family when things began to get hard.

walk out with **salir con (el novio, la novia):** He asked her if she would like to walk out with him.

walk over **atravesar a pie:** The tramp walked over the bridge and sat down to rest.
derrotar fácilmente: The Birmingham team walked over our team in the recent match.
pisotear (los sentimientos de alguien): She just lets her husband walk all over her as he likes.
acompañar (andando): I'll walk you over to your office.

walk through **atravesar andando:** Young girls are advised against walking through the forest alone.

walk up **subir andando:** We had to walk up because the lift was out of order.

walk up to **acercarse con un motivo:** To our astonishment she just walked up to the great man and asked him for an autograph.

warm up **calentarse:** The gymnasts were warming up before the performance began.
animar: This party is very dull; let's warm it up a little.
calentar: Warm this water up, please.

wash away **llevarse (el agua):** The tide washed away all traces of the barbecue on the beach.
quitar lavando: She carefully washed the dirt away from around the wound.

wash back **devolver (el mar):** The body, which had been in the sea all night, was washed back on the beach.

wash down **lavar echando agua:** He spends two hours every Sunday washing down the car.

wash off **quitar lavando:** The shopkeeper was trying to wash off the slogans painted on the walls of his shop.

wash out **quitar lavando:** Can these stains be washed out with ordinary detergent?
estropearse (un festejo): Heavy rain over the weekend washed out the race meeting.

wash over **batir (las olas):** The waves gently washed over the rocks near the shore.

wash up **lavar (la vajilla):** Mary washes up and her husband dries the dishes.
traer (las olas): A bottle with a message was washed up on the beach.

waste away **consumirse:** When he had fever he wasted away to a shadow of himself.

watch for **acechar:** The robbers watched for the traveller coming along the road.

watch out **vigilar:** They were told to watch out lest they fell into temptation.
tener cuidado: Everybody shouted: "Watch out!" when the stone fell from the building.

watch out for **tener cuidado con:** Postmen watch out for dogs that attack without warning.

watch over **proteger:** In her prayers the little girl asked God to watch over her brother and sisters.
vigilar: The alert guard sat with a shotgun watching over the money.

water down **aguar (un licor):** As the whisky was very strong we had to water it down.

wave aside **rechazar (con un gesto de la mano):** The marathon runner waved aside all offers of help as he stumbled for the finishing line.

wear away **desgastar:** The action of the waves wore away the foundations of the lighthouse.

wear down **desgastarse:** The spindle wore down to half its size through constant use.

cansar, agotar: Constant attacks gradually wore down the defenders' resistance.

wear off **pasarse (un dolor):** After taking two aspirins the pain slowly wore off.
quitarse (por uso o roce): The paint of the door soon wore off.
perder fuerza: That first impression did not wear off until they met again a week later.

wear on **pasar lentamente (el tiempo):** As the time wore on we got used to the noise.

wear out **agotarse (una persona):** The work in the shop is slowly wearing her out.
cansar: I always feel worn out in the morning.
desgastar: Jimmy always wears out his shoes quickly.

wear up **gastar una prenda (antes de comprar otra):** I'll wear up this jersey before I buy a new one I saw in Selfridges.

weep away **continuar llorando:** She wept away silently as she listened to the sad news.

weigh out **pesar (cantidades):** Do you remember when the shopkeeper used to weigh out the tea and sugar in the shop?

weigh up **sopesar:** After carefully weighing up the situation, he decided there was nothing he could do.

while away **matar (el tiempo):** She whiled away the afternoon lying on the sofa reading a novel.

whip off **quitarse (una prenda de un tirón):** She whipped off her apron and tidied her hair before going to answer the door.

whip up **batir:** Mary whipped the cream up and put it in the fridge to cool.

win back **recuperar:** I wonder what I can do to win my husband back, said Mrs Wilson.

win out **salir victorioso:** I'm sure you'll win out in spite of all difficulties.

win over **ganar (para una causa):** He is such a persuasive talker that he could win a lot of people over to his cause.

win through **salir vencedor (de dificultades):** After many years of effort he won through and got a top job.

wind off **desenrollar (una madeja):** Before you begin knitting, you must wind the wool off the skein.

wind up **enrollar:** She wound up the tape and put it on a shelf.
dar cuerda (a una maquinaria): Don't forget to wind up the clock before you go to bed.
finalizar: The party finally wound up at about four in the morning.

wink at **hacer la vista gorda a:** The boss winks at all Peter's faults, as he is his favourite.

wipe away **enjugar:** She surreptitiously wiped a few tears away.

wipe off **liquidar (una deuda):** Thanks to the money they received, they were able to wipe off all their debts.
quitar (con un paño): The teacher told Tim to wipe off the words on the blackboard.

wipe out **limpiar (con un paño):** She wiped the bath out and opened the window.
aniquilar: The enemy were wiped out to the last man.

wipe up **enjugar:** The barman wiped up the beer that the drunk had spilled.

work away **trabajar con ahínco:** They all worked away hard until they heard the clock strike five.

work in **introducir:** In his speech the Prime Minister worked in a reference to the recent council elections.

work in with **encajar con:** I'm not sure that your idea can work in with what we have in mind.

work into **introducir en (con dificultad):** The plumber worked his finger into the tube to see if he could find the blockage.

work off **trabajar (para saldar una deuda):** They spent the rest of their lives working off the debt.

work out **agotarse (una mina):** The mine was worked out in the last decade.
calcular: Can you work out the cost of two tons of coal at six pounds a hundredweight?
resolver (un problema): We worked out the answer to the problem without trouble.
planear: What do you think he is working out in that head of his?
resultar: Everything worked out better than we expected.

work up **excitarse:** The doctor told the woman not to get worked up or angry.
levantar (un negocio): Old Hyman worked the firm up from nothing.

work up into **transformarse mediante fabricación:** This silk will work up into very good fabrics.

wrap up **taparse (abrigarse):** She was so wrapped up against the cold that only her nose was visible.
envolver: The goods were all wrapped up in fancy paper.
ocultar: He wrapped up his meaning in euphemistic expressions.

wring off **retorcer:** The cruel man wrung the chicken's head off.

wring out **escurrir retorciendo:** After she had washed the blankets, she wrung them out.

wrinkle up **arrugar:** Johnny wrinkled his brow up in concentration.

write away **escribir diligentemente:** The novelist wrote away every night until daybreak.

write back **contestar por escrito:** When she applied for the job, the firm wrote back asking her for an interview.

write down **anotar:** The students wrote down what the lecturer was saying.
tachar (a alguien de algo): Before he knew her well, he had written her down as a snob.
apuntar: I like to write my ideas down at once, before I can forget them.

write in **insertar (palabras):** The pupils were asked to write words in the blank spaces.
enviar cartas: Members of the public often write in to the television company asking questions about this programme.

write off **escribir sin dilación (una carta):** Write off asking them about the money!
cancelar (una deuda): The shopkeeper kindly wrote off their debt.
descartar: They had already written him off as a failure.

write off to **escribir sin dilación a:** All the candidates wrote off to the firm asking about the interview.

write on **continuar escribiendo:** The secretary wrote on until the boss told her to stop.

write out **poner un escrito en limpio:** Could you write these notes out more clearly?
escribir con todo detalle: He wrote out all the details in his best handwriting.

write round **escribir a mucha gente:** When they moved, they wrote round to give all their friends their new address.

write up **ensalzar por escrito:** The critics wrote the play up well in the papers.

ampliar notas: Students should write up their lesson notes in the evening.
poner al día: The captain sat down to write up the log for the day.
escribir (algo) en un lugar elevado. The teacher wrote the winner's name up on the blackboard.

Exercises

Divididos en tres secciones, los ejercicios que se presentan a continuación, hacen un estudio comparado de las distintas partículas de que van acompañados los *Phrasal Verbs.*

1

En esta sección se da a elegir entre 2 partículas (preposiciones o adverbios). Rellénense los espacios en blanco, de forma que las oraciones tengan sentido.

EXERCISE 1

in, into

1. She went .... the house and shut the door.
2. He laid .... the assailant and left him begging for mercy.
3. Jack looked ....on his way home last night.
4. When are you moving .... your new house?
5. She looked .... the bag to see if it was empty.
6. We went to visit our new neighbours when they moved ....
7. She invited him to come .... and have a cup of coffee.
8. Night was setting .... as my father took the road leading to the coast.
9. Heat turns water .... steam.
10. Mrs Green brought the geraniums ....as the night was cold.

****

EXERCISE 2

on, over

1. We always talk things .... before making a decision.
2. All the travellers hurried .... to reach the hotel before nightfall.
3. Richard jumped .... the bus as it was about to start.
4. He jumped .... the stream without wetting his feet.
5. The cow kicked .... the milking pail and spilled the milk.
6. As he was entering the shed he knocked his head .... a beam.
7. She leaned her head .... the young man's shoulder.
8. The match was .... at five o'clock.
9. Let's go .... the lesson once more.
10. Jill fitted the shoes .... before she bought them.

EXERCISE 3

on, in

1. All the pupils looked .... their teacher as a friend.
2. The lid of the box was pushed .... by the weight of the stones on top.
3. The policeman told the onlookers to move ....
4. The heirloom was passed .... from father to son.
5. The children played .... until it was time for tea.
6. Come .... and see the show!
7. The car pulled .... and a beautiful woman got out.
8. Bruce pulled .... his coat and left in a hurry.
9. Mrs. Williams called the children .... to have their dinner.
10. This door opens ...., not out.

****

EXERCISE 4

on, off

1. I told him to get on the number forty-five bus and to get .... at Marble Arch.
2. The Wilsons are getting the electricity laid .... soon.
3. Bill went .... working after the others had left.
4. Tom hurried .... to meet his girl-friend, his mind happy.
5. Keep .... the grass.
6. The heavy blow knocked the man .... the ladder.
7. Jim was knocking .... the door for a long time before it opened.
8. At that moment a N° 35 bus came along, so I jumped .... it.
9. The girls kept .... talking after Miss Smith told them to stop.
10. The old man walked .... without saying goodbye.

****

EXERCISE 5

about, away

1. The cowboy pushed ...... the glass and turned to face the strangers.
2. When the bright light hurt his eyes, he looked ....
3. The couple ran .... to Scotland to get married.
4. They were fighting .... a cat which each of them claimed to own.
5. You know, that's something I've never thought ....!

6. The rich man locked the jewels .... in the safe.
7. He's always talking .... the time he was in Greenland.
8. How do the Eskimos while .... the time in Greenland?
9. She was still talking .... after the last of the guests had left.
10. As he was going .... I noticed that he limped slightly.

****

EXERCISE 6

out, off

1. Green & Co. are moving .... by the end of the month.
2. He knocked the dottle .... of the pipe by tapping it against a stone.
3. When he knocked .... work, his girl-friend was waiting for him at the factory gate.
4. As the car moved slowly .... a hand waved farewell from the window.
5. Although written .... as useless, he surprised us by succeeding in the job.
6. There was a large notice which warned us to keep .... the lawns.
7. There was a high fence around the garden to keep trespassers ......
8. They haven't spoken a word to each other since they fell ....
9. When asked where he got his television set, he always said it fell .... the back of a lorry.
10. She put .... the light and settled down to sleep.

****

EXERCISE 7

under, down

1. It is difficult to live a scandal ....
2. The firm went .... due to bad management.
3. She slammed .... the receiver and continued reading.
4. He was still .... the effects of the drugs when they visited him in hospital.
5. Smith was sent .... from university for punching Mr Jones.
6. Every night before she sleeps, she glances .... the bed for fear of a mouse.
7. It annoyed her when he talked .... to her as if she were new in the office.
8. Take .... the suitcases; the next stop is ours!
9. The dangerous prisoner was put .... guard and sent for trial.

10. The rain came .... in bucketfuls and inundated the fields.

EXERCISE 8

through, back

1. We saw .... him the moment he opened his mouth.
2. He offered his apologies and took .... everything he said.
3. It was only his tremendous courage that saw him .... his long illness.
4. His belief in his own abilities carried him ....
5. To count .... from 100 to one is not so easy as it seems.
6. The force of the explosion threw him .... against the wall.
7. After many years of effort, he won .... and got a top job.
8. He sat up all night at the card table to win .... some of the money he had lost.
9. When he applied for the post, the firm wrote .... saying they were sorry.
10. I rang asking to be put .... to Mr Hartley.

****

EXERCISE 9

over, out

1. The house looked a mess when the party was ....
2. A term of trial often brings .... the best in some people.
3. He called .... loudly in the empty house, but there was no answer.
4. Look .... There's a car coming!
5. He jumped .... the stream without wetting his feet.
6. It's an unpleasant job to clean .... a public lavatory.
7. Her brother used to watch .... her investments.
8. The parachutist jumped .... of the plane.
9. Suddenly a ball came flying .... the wall.
10. Redhaired people stand .... in a crowd.

****

EXERCISE 10

across, through

1. She went .... the field and into the thicket.
2. As we were coming .... the wood, we saw an old man picking mushrooms.

3. The dressmaker cut .... the cloth.
4. I'd been looking for it for a long time till I came .... it by chance.
5. Negotiations fell .... and the strike continued.
6. A high-velocity bullet can go .... a brick wall.
7. Let's go .... the street, to the sunny side.
8. The boat passed slowly .... the lake.
9. We passed .... the doorway and entered the gloomy house.
10. He pulled .... well after his last illness.

---

2 *En esta sección se proponen ejercicios en los que se da a elegir entre 3 partículas. Complétense las frases con las mismas.*

EXERCISE 11

for, by, along

1. How will you account .... such a big difference?
2. I pass .... the cinema on my way to work.
3. I've come .... the book you promised to lend me.
4. The railway workers stood .... the tracks as the trains passed.
5. He was hurrying .... not looking where he was going.
6. How did you come .... these jewels?
7. The policemen were told to stand .... and await further orders.
8. The woman went .... her assailant with an umbrella.
9. The boxer ran .... the roadway jabbing the air.
10. The years rolled .... and Jack Roberts didn't get any younger.

****

EXERCISE 12

into, up, over

1. Exposure to heat turns ice .... water.
2. You've rubbed him .... the wrong way and now he's angry with us.
3. John turned his eyes .... and said he would be incapable of such a deed.
4. I changed my American dollars .... euros at the airport.
5. The holidays are ...., so it's back to work again!
6. Can you see .... the top of that wall?

7. The critics wrote the new play .... well in the newspaper.
8. When are they moving .... their new house?
9. These matters will have to stand .... until the next meeting.
10. I can't put .... with Tim; he's always complaining.

****

EXERCISE 13

at, after, on

1. We knew what he was driving .... when he said he was broke.
2. His blindness was brought .... by too much study.
3. The dog went .... the sheep running and barking.
4. She seems to be an irritable person; she's always shouting .... her children.
5. He reckoned .... earning thirty dollars for the job, but he only got twenty.
6. The dog rushed .... the tramp, but stopped short when it saw the stick.
7. He told us not to worry because he could look .... himself.
8. Don't forget to call .... us the next time you are in town.
9. It suddenly dawned .... him that the girl really liked him.
10. Have Vincent and Christine settled .... a date for their wedding?

******

EXERCISE 14

out, down, back

1. The tent flaps were held .... with pegs which were driven into the ground.
2. The examiner handed .... the papers at the beginning of the exam.
3. Keep .... all expenses till we are clear of debt.
4. A blast of heat when the oven door was opened made him step .... hastily.
5. He helped the invalid .... of the car.
6. The haughty cavalier flung .... a gauntlet as a challenge.
7. She sent .... all his love-letters unopened.
8. Are you going .... tonight, or do you prefer to stay at home?

EXERCISE 15

round, about, along

1. She heard voices and looked .... to see who it was.
2. As he seemed to know the way and moreover, he had a flashlight, we went .... with him.
3. They were told to stop fooling .... and get on with their work.
4. Won't you come .... and see us some day next week?
5. He felt .... on the table to find his glasses.
6. They told her they would send the goods .... to her house that very day.
7. It was ten minutes before the boxer came .... after being knocked out.
8. Let's go .... and see how Aunt Doll is keeping.
9. When the boss came in, he ordered the chattering typists to get .... their work at once.

******

EXERCISE 16

under, over, away

1. When the party was .... there was a lot to be done.
2. The two dogs sprang .... playfully and circled each other.
3. When he took his hand .... from his lips, it was blood stained.
4. The cat got .... the fence and out of the garden.
5. The meeting of the sports club has been held .... until next week.
6. The crocodile killed the antelope by holding its head .... the water.
7. The picnickers lit a fire in the hope that the smoke would keep .... the clouds of gnats.
8. When old Jones died, his son took ...... the running of the company.
9. The beautiful princess lay as if dead in the glass coffin .... an evil spell.
10. When a person dies it is often euphemistically said that he has passed ....

EXERCISE 17

in, out, through

1. Can you go .... this letter, Miss Smith, and check for mistakes?
2. They plan to see the old year .... in the Bahamas.
3. Bring the bicycle .... with you and don't leave it outside!
4. That's our new house. Look .... and see if you like it.
5. Can you put me .... to Mr Armstrong, please?
6. I'm sorry, sir; I'm afraid we're completely .... of Pear's soap.
7. Robert Brown suffered a severe depression when his girlfriend declared they were ....
8. Mrs White took .... the washing as it began to rain.
9. Johnny's mother told him he had to be .... by eight o'clock.
10. He held .... his hand and declared how pleased he was to see me.

******

EXERCISE 18

on, off, by

1. A good friend will stand .... you in time of need.
2. It is a good idea to put some money .... for a rainy day.
3. He switched the television .... and sat down to watch.
4. The police wanted to know how he had come .... the radio he had in his hand.
5. If you stand .... your toes you can just see over the top of the hedge.
6. The train went .... the rails and turned over .
7. A cool head will help you to get .... at difficult moments.
8. A section of the road was marked .... for taxis.
9. She put him .... with a vague promise of meeting him the following week.
10. The dog rolled .... the soft grass of the lawn.

******

EXERCISE 19

over, across, back

1. I'd been looking for it for a long time till I came .... it by chance.
2. Put that watch .... where you found it; it belongs to Jack.
3. The dog came running .... with the pheasant in its mouth.
4. The less important points were held .... until the next meeting.

5. She comes .... very well on television.
6. The barman pushed the glass of beer .... the countertop to the customer .
7. She was about to blurt everything out, but she bit .... her words.
8. The milk spilled .... the edge of the saucepan.
9. I can't get it .... to them that the period of plenty has ended.
10. The little boy hit .... at the bully who had caught him by the neck.

******

EXERCISE 20

up, down, upon

1. I hope someone hits .... an alternative to petrol.
2. What you say may be taken .... and used in evidence.
3. Do you think this medicine will act .... his nerves?
4. He took a book .... from the shelf and opened it at random.
5. The bank robbers made the employees put their hands ....
6. The irate mother told the children to shut .... as she had a headache.
7. I suddenly came .... the answer when I least expected it.
8. A smart car drew .... and a well-dressed woman got out.
9. The tired, irritable boy threw .... the book and declared he could never understand mathematics.
10. Turn .... the radio, please. I can't hear what they are saying.

3

En esta sección, se han de rellenar los espacios en blanco con la partícula apropiada, tras elegir entre varias. El número que aparece entre paréntesis junto a algunas partículas, indica las veces que dicha partícula debe emplearse en el ejercicio. Obsérvese que los ejercicios 27 y 28 son dos "mini-relatos."

EXERCISE 21

over, in(2), away, about, up(2), out

1. A part of the snow-laden roof fell .... during our absence.
2. The majestic-looking stallion reared .... fiercely on its hind legs.
3. When I told James I had some questions to ask, he lit his pipe and said, 'Fire. .... !'
4. All the candidates wrote ...... to the firm asking about the interview.

5. Peter Jones came .... with the solution to the problem.
6. Who's going to see .... the preparations for the party?
7. Mr Scott glanced rapidly .... the report, stopping only to underline two items.
8. The flame flickered for an instant and went ...., leaving us in complete darkness.

******

EXERCISE 22

down, without, into, for, over, up, away, out

1. The notice was pinned .... for all to see.
2. Obediently, the students took .... all their lecturer said.
3. He had no money to buy cigarettes and had to do .... a smoke the whole weekend.
4. Molly does .... a wealthy family in Battersea; in other words, she scrubs their floor and cooks their meals.
5. The report goes .... the social aspect very thoroughly.
6. The irate parents told the lad to stay .... from their daughter.
7. It wasn't much of a story but he spun it .... for ten minutes.
8. Once the crisis was .... life became normal again.

******

EXERCISE 23

up, away, off, through, back, over, out

1. When he was young he used to sleep whole mornings ....
2. I can soon get a quick snack .... for you if you're hungry after the show.
3. If the mixture gets too thick, stir it .... with this stick.
4. He walked angrily .... without another word.
5. If your watch is fast, you'll simply have to put it ....
6. Professor Stacey tends to spoil his lectures by drawing them .... too much.
7. He just managed to get .... the narrow opening without touching the projecting cable.
8. I don't like people standing .... me while I'm working.

EXERCISE 24

down, out, up, off, away, back, over, to

1. Nobody can make .... what's wrong with Roger; he's been acting queerly lately.
2. The tramp grabbed the goose and made .... with it before the astonished gaze of the housewife.
3. They were ordered to clean .... the mess they had made.
4. The burglars made .... with all our silver.
5. Hey! Just a minute! Slow ...., can't you? You're going too fast for us.
6. Hugh threw his head .... and laughed heartily when he heard the joke.
7. We went .... several houses before deciding on this one.
8. We're eagerly looking forward .... your party.

******

EXERCISE 25

over, back, down, off, in, out, across, up, about, along

1. When are you going to try .... your new motorbike?
2. How much did you have to lay .... as a deposit for your house?
3. She lit a fire in the grate to warm ...... the room before Bob arrived.
4. I wish Jim would not fool .... so much.
5. Change the battery when your watch begins to run ....
6. Ann will take .... when your turn finishes.
7. The mob began to fall .... before the police.
8. The woman took .... the curtains prior to cleaning the window.
9. The aeroplane took .... on schedule.
10. Drop .... and see us one day.

******

EXERCISE 26

by, on, out, down, for, to, up, at, over, off

1. Peggy blew .... at the suggestion that she might have been in love with someone else before.
2. Mr Richards told the chauffeur to drive .... when he saw the hitch-hikers.
3. He told the men they could knock ......when they'd finished the job.
4. He is one of those people who simply live .... their work.

5. On his first visit to Brazil he was struck .... with fever.
6. As he was friendless, he had no one to turn .... for advice.
7. His work was so tiring that by six o' clock he was worn ....
8. The rain is giving .... Now we can start our journey.
9. During his long working life he laid several thousand pounds ....
10. A chance like that is something I would jump ....!

******

EXERCISE 27

up, out(2), along, on, through, down, to, off, for

The Boxer

1. A right uppercut knocked the boxer .... and he lay still on the canvas.
2. Despite the frantic efforts of his seconds, he did not come ....
3. Willing hands helped the seconds to carry the stunned boxer .... of the ring.
4. Somebody had sent .... an ambulance, which was ready and waiting.
5. The unconscious pugilist was laid .... on a stretcher and placed in the ambulance.
6. The white-coated attendants entered, slamming the doors, and the ambulance drove ....
7. Luckily there was little traffic that night so they were not held .... and they reached the hospital quickly.
8. In the hospital, the stretcher was placed on a trolley and rushed .... the corridor.
9. The surgeon drew .... his long transparent gloves and operated on the prize-fighter.
10. Despite the seriousness of his injury, he pulled ...., but now he no longer boxes.

******

EXERCISE 28

around, round, down(2), up, into, away, back, in, on

In the Far West

1. The red disk of the sun had just gone .... behind the foothills when the stranger rode into town.

2. He dismounted before the saloon, hitched his horse and drew himself .... to his full height of six feet three.
3. He pushed the door of the bar open and stepped ....
4. The assembled drinkers at the bar counter drew .... to leave him room.
5. He ordered a double whisky, which he drank .... in one gulp.
6. Ordering another drink, he looked ....
7. His eyes fell......... a tall man in a far corner.
8. Pushing .... the glass, he strode to the centre of the saloon, calling the other man's name.
9. On hearing his name, the latter looked ......, a smile parting his lips.
10. The two men rushed to meet, falling .... each other's arms, murmuring 'brother!'

Answer Key

EXERCISE 1
1. into. **2.** into. **3.** in. **4.** into. **5.** into. **6.** in. **7.** in. **8.** in. **9.** into. **10.** in.

EXERCISE 2
1. over. **2.** on. **3.** on. **4.** over. **5.** over. **6.** on. **7.** on. **8.** over. **9.** over. **10.** on.

EXERCISE 3
1. on. **2.** in. **3.** on. **4.** on. **5.** on. **6.** in. **7.** in. **8.** on. **9.** in. **10.** in.

EXERCISE 4
1. off. **2.** on. **3.** on. **4.** off. **5.** off. **6.** off. **7.** on. **8.** on. **9.** on. **10.** off.

EXERCISE 5
1. away. **2.** away. **3.** away. **4.** about. **5.** about. **6.** away. **7.** about. **8.** away. **9.** away. **10.** away.

EXERCISE 6
1. out. **2.** out. **3.** off. **4.** off. **5.** off. **6.** off. **7.** out. **8.** out. **9.** off. **10.** out.

EXERCISE 7
1. down. **2.** under. **3.** down. **4.** under. **5.** down. **6.** under. **7.** down. **8.** down. **9.** under. **10.** down.

EXERCISE 8
1. through. **2.** back. **3.** through. **4.** through. **5.** back. **6.** back. **7.** through. **8.** back. **9.** back. **10.** through.

EXERCISE 9
1. over. **2.** out. **3.** out. **4.** out. **5.** over. **6.** out. **7.** over. **8.** out. **9.** over. **10.** out.

EXERCISE 10
1. across. **2.** through. **3.** through. **4.** across. **5.** through. **6.** through. **7.** across. **8.** across. **9.** through. **10.** through.

EXERCISE 11
1. for. **2.** by. **3.** for. **4.** along. **5.** along. **6.** by. **7.** by. **8.** for. **9.** along. **10.** by.

EXERCISE 12
1. into. **2.** up. **3.** up. **4.** into. **5.** over. **6.** over. **7.** up. **8.** into. **9.** over. **10.** up.

EXERCISE 13
1. at. **2.** on. **3.** after. **4.** at. **5.** on. **6.** at. **7.** after. **8.** on. **9.** on. **10.** on.

EXERCISE 14
1. down. **2.** out. **3.** down. **4.** back. **5.** out. **6.** down. **7.** back. **8.** out.

EXERCISE 15
1. round. **2.** along. **3.** about. **4.** round. **5.** about. **6.** along. **7.** round. **8.** round. **9.** about.

EXERCISE 16
1. over. **2.** away. **3.** away. **4.** under. **5.** over. **6.** under. **7.** away. **8.** over. **9.** under. **10.** away.

EXERCISE 17
1. through. **2.** out. **3.** in. **4.** in. **5.** through. **6.** out. **7.** through. **8.** in. **9.** in. **10.** out.

EXERCISE 18
1. by. **2.** by. **3.** on. **4.** by. **5.** on. **6.** off. **7.** by. **8.** off. **9.** off. **10.** on.

EXERCISE 19
1. across. **2.** back. **3.** back. **4.** over. **5.** across. **6.** across. **7.** back. **8.** over. **9.** across. **10.** back.

EXERCISE 20
1. upon. **2.** down. **3.** upon. **4.** down. **5.** up. **6.** up. **7.** upon. **8.** up. **9.** down. **10.** up.

EXERCISE 21
1. in. **2.** up. **3.** away. **4.** in. **5.** up. **6.** about. **7.** over. **8.** out.

EXERCISE 22
1. up. **2.** down. **3.** without. **4.** for. **5.** into. **6.** away. **7.** out. **8.** over.

EXERCISE 23
1. away. **2.** up. **3.** up. **4.** off. **5.** back. **6.** out. **7.** through. **8.** over.

EXERCISE 24
1. out. **2.** away/off. **3.** up. **4.** away/off. **5.** down. **6.** back. **7.** over. **8.** to.

EXERCISE 25
1. out. **2.** down. **3.** up. **4.** about. **5.** down. **6.** over. **7.** back. **8.** down. **9.** off. **10.** in.

EXERCISE 26
1. up. **2.** on. **3.** off. **4.** for. **5.** down. **6.** to. **7.** out. **8.** over. **9.** by. **10.** at.

EXERCISE 27
1. out. **2.** to. **3.** out. **4.** for. **5.** down. **6.** off. **7.** up. **8.** along. **9.** on. **10.** through.

EXERCISE 28
1. down. **2.** up. **3.** in. **4.** back. **5.** down. **6.** around. **7.** on. **8.** away. **9.** round. **10.** into.

From the same publisher

Libros didácticos complementarios - Resource Material

GRAMMAR & REFERENCE BOOKS

El inglés compendiado. An Easy English Grammar. Manual muy completo, claro, práctico y esquemático de gramática inglesa. Se complementa con el libro "Cuaderno de ejercicios en inglés. Práctica de gramática y estructuras."

Las preposiciones inglesas y sus ejercicios. La información recopilada en este libro no se encuentra como tal en ningún tratado de gramática. Abundantes frases prácticas, 35 ejercicios y soluciones.

Las dificultades idiomáticas del inglés. Resuelve de manera muy práctica las dificultades lingüísticas que con que se encuentran los estudiantes de inglés con mayor frecuencia.

To Get. El verbo comodín del inglés. Estudio completo y sumamente práctico de este verbo. Con 25 ejercicios y soluciones.

Sinónimos ingleses explicados. English Synonyms Explained. Cuando un estudiante de inglés busca en el diccionario una palabra, p.ej. "mirar" encuentra: *Glance, Stare, Contemplate, Gaze, Watch, etc.* ¿Cuál elegir? Este libro explica cada palabra desde un punto de vista práctico.

EXERCISES & TESTS

100 tests para reavivar su inglés. Selección de 100 Tests muy variados, divididos en tres niveles: elemental, intermedio y avanzado. Con soluciones.

PRACTICE IN TRANSLATION SPANISH-ENGLISH.

Manual práctico de traducción inversa. Español-inglés. Contiene más de 1.000 ejercicios de traducción del español al inglés, desde la frase al texto. Con alternativas.

Textos literarios para traducir. Español-inglés. Nivel avanzado. Textos literarios de autores contemporáneos de habla española traducidos al inglés con numerosas notas y variantes alternativas. Muy útil para alumnos avanzados y opositores.

SPECIALIZED DICTIONARIES

Catálogo de expresiones para la traducción inversa. Español - Inglés. Más de 7.000 expresiones de uso corriente que facilitan tanto la expresión oral como escrita.

Spanish Words & English Meanings. Español-Inglés.

De cada palabra española se hace un estudio de sus significados y matices, dando para cada uno el equivalente en inglés. P.ej.: COLA: de un animal=tail; de un avión=tail, de un vestido=train; fila=queu; etc Así se estudian numerosísimas palabras del lenguaje corriente.

Diccionario auxiliar del traductor. Español-inglés. The Translator's Auxiliary Dictionary. Más de 5.000 frases de uso corriente para ilustrar el uso de las palabras del lenguaje cotidiano.

English False Friends. Palabras inglesas engañosas. Selección de palabras inglesas cuyo parecido con otras españolas es motivo de equivocaciones. Con ejercicios y soluciones.

Diccionario de dudas del inglés. Diccionario excepcional que analiza y resuelve las dudas del estudiante español.

ENGLISH PRONUNCIATION BOOKS

La pronunciación inglesa. Fonética y fonología. A Handbook of English Pronunciation. (Con Cassette). (9ª ed.) Estudio práctico de los sonidos ingleses. Ilustrado con 50 dibujos y 10 fotos. Nivel básico.

MISCELLANEOUS ENGLISH

Refranes ingleses para estudiantes de inglés. Selección de 500 refranes ingleses. Incluye: su traducción o equivalencia en español, interpretación, puntos lingüísticos, ideas afines y notas. Se completa con 32 ejercicios y soluciones.

Grammar & Humour. Aprenda inglés con una sonrisa. Antología del humor británico. Con breves comentarios gramaticales. Ejercicios y soluciones.

English in Flashes. Inglés en formato breve. Más de 300 puntos lingüísticos ingleses de uso corriente y de diversa dificultad.

Catálogo Gratuito

Solicite gratuitamente nuestro catálogo completo y totalmente actualizado de *Libros Didácticos Complementarios – Resource Material* escribiendo a la siguiente dirección, o llamando al teléfono que se indica.

Anglo-Didáctica Publishing
C/ Santiago de Compostela, 16 – bajo B
28034 Madrid. España
Tel y Fax: (34) 91 378 01 88
email: anamerino@worldonline.es